TRACE

WILL YOU BE THE ONE?

Touching the hearts of teachers, changing the lives of children with challenging behaviour

Be the One Press
A division of **Be the One Transforming Behaviour Ltd**
PO Box 70258, London, N4 9DR

A CIP catalogue record of this book is available from the British Library

ISBN 978-0-9575302-0-1

This book is a work of non-fiction, however, some of the names, dates, personal details and places have been changed in order to protect the identities of those mentioned in any real-life accounts.

Edited by Jacqueline Burns at London Writers' Club

Text and cover design by David Eldridge and Holly Giblin at Two Associates
Illustrations by Tom Pearce at Drawings of Things
Photography by Leroy Harley

Printed and bound in the UK by Berforts Information Press Ltd.

2 4 6 8 10 9 7 5 3 1

For Mary, the One who said yes

Contents:

Acknowledgements

The truth is that I am simply a product of the Ones who I have been blessed enough to meet along my journey and it is now my privilege to name and thank some of them…

Thanks to my mum, you have always encouraged me to chase my dreams and completion of this book is one of them.

To Mary Id Boukariane for taking that bold step all those years ago. I will never forget what you did for me. You gave me a story to tell – I hope I can leave a similar legacy. Your help with proofreading was also greatly appreciated.

To Nina Brown, thank you for being such an important part of my story. More than twenty years later here we are! Thank you for your support and advice. You are a treasured friend.

Thanks to Dawn Ferdinand for providing a picture of passion, leadership and excellence. We have come a long way since the interview in the ICT suite! Your help with proofreading was invaluable.

To Jamela Ricketts for her support and encouragement throughout this writing process. Your sincerity, honesty and commitment to the vision are greatly appreciated. You are a true friend.

To my mentor Lela Kogbara. I'm not sure if you remember back in 2007 when you helped me to flesh out exactly what 'Will You be the One?' was about? But I have never forgotten. Thank you for getting me started.

To my coach Grace Owen for her insight and wisdom. Thank you for keeping me focused and for spurring me on. I'm quite sure I could not have done it without you.

Marlon Smith, thank you so much for the constant 'check-ins' to ensure I was on track. I have really valued your support and advice.

To Doug Williams for your help with proofreading and for having a ready smile any time we talked about the progress of the book. Thank you for being one of the Ones.

To Martha Braithwaite, Jenny Lewis and Caroline King, thank you for your ongoing interest in the book and for your sense of anticipation and excitement as I neared completion.

Thank you to the wonderful team at St Mark's Primary School for being so receptive to the first ever 'Will You be the One?' training session. Little did we know what we were starting…

To my editor Jacqueline Burns for your enthusiasm and support throughout this process. Your belief in this book has meant a great deal. Thank you to Emma Rose for an outstanding job with the copyedit.

Thanks to David Eldridge and Holly Giblin for the cover and text design and Tom Pearce for the illustrations.

To all of the wonderful children that I have had the pleasure of working with over the years, thank you for being a part of my life and for allowing me to be a part of yours.

To the readers of Will You be the One?, I hope this book encourages you to do all that you can for the children in your care.

Introduction

Little did I know,
she was the One

School Antics, London, 1988
My friend had brought a black miniskirt into school. After lunch she dared me to walk into class wearing it over my uniform. Groups of girls gathered around me, sniggering as I wriggled myself into the tube-like skirt, rolled my uniform skirt right up to my waist and strutted into afternoon registration.

The whole class erupted into laughter; my classmates hysterically rolled around in their seats. The sound of their laughter filled me with euphoria. It was a sound that girls like me loved to hear: the sound of popularity, the sound of attention, the sound of belonging. I triumphantly sat down in my seat. I'd successfully disrupted the session and at the same time elevated myself in the ranks to class clown. My form tutor, however, didn't find it funny at all and wasted no time in expressing her disgust at my behaviour.

'How dare you come in here and cause such disruption!' she bellowed, banging her hand on the table. She continued, 'how dare you take up my time with such nonsense!'

It was the unexpected sound of her voice cracking with these last words that made me look up. I didn't want it to be true but the tears that trickled down her cheeks were real. Like the smell of fresh paint, her pain filled the room. It covered the walls and no one dared move lest they became tainted. It didn't matter whether I moved or sat still, I was guilty. I may as well have been holding a tin and a brush. Her pain was my doing.

I sat there trying hard not to allow the feelings of guilt to show on my face. There was no way I could make it known that I felt regret; that just didn't fit my image. It bothered me that I had made her cry because I'd not wanted that, and besides, at the time I felt that for a teacher she was okay.

From that day on, registration just didn't feel the same. It was like having to revisit the scene of a crime I'd committed again and again. For weeks I laid low because I felt embarrassed about what I had done. I avoided eye contact and made the effort not to be in close proximity to her. Several weeks passed, but eventually the day came when she caught up with me. I had no idea just how significant that day would be...

I hadn't even noticed her standing there. I'd escaped my French lesson, but my relief at skipping ten minutes of class vanished with the sound of her voice. Shivers of regret shot down my spine.

'Can I speak to you?' she asked. I still remember how awkward I felt; I didn't know where to look. What did she want to talk to me about? I looked straight past her, my voice sounding feeble as I said, 'I've just been to the toilet Miss. I need to get back to my lesson.'

'I would like to speak with you,' she said, this time with a touch more coercion as she gestured towards her office door.

The memory of the distress I'd caused that day swiftly moved to the front of my mind. Not wanting to create further hurt, I reluctantly followed her to the office.

The click of the door shutting behind me made me feel nauseous and I refused her offer of a seat. But the question that followed was both unexpected and has stayed with me all these years since. More to the point, even now, the answer to that question fills me with a multitude of feelings that I struggle to describe.

'Do you know what I spend my break times doing?' she began. Certain it was a rhetorical question I just looked at her, eyebrows raised. She continued. 'I defend you in the staffroom.' A single bead of sweat trickled down my spine.

Having convinced myself I was going to be facing a serious dressing-down for the miniskirt episode, I was completely unprepared for the disclosure that followed.

'A lot of teachers here think you are not going to amount to very much. They say that you will never get past your negative attitude and aggression.' My head was spinning: the closed door, the small space and the reality of what they thought of me – it was all too much. I was dying to get out of there. But there was more.

'Whenever you get into trouble I think, why does she only show them that side of her? You are a leader; you have so much influence around here. At least that's what I see. Every time they criticise you in the staffroom, that's what I tell them. Sometimes the choices you make really disappoint me because I don't know if you realise what is inside you. You have huge amounts of potential, but you have got to get your behaviour in check.' Her voice was soft and sincere. It was certainly not the telling off that I had feared.

I was staggered by what I was hearing. Surely she wasn't talking about me, after everything I had done?

'I would like to make myself available to you every Thursday after school for a chat. Only if you want to. I will be here and you can come for half an hour just to chat.' She made a point of making eye contact as she concluded, 'I'd like to help Tracey.'

I didn't accept the offer, neither did I reject it; I was simply trying to take it all in. I left the room thinking, *she called me into her office to tell me I was a leader, to tell me that I was a person of influence, to tell me that she believed in me so much that she stood up for me in the staffroom.* Not once did she mention the fact that only a few weeks ago I had reduced her to tears.

I also left that room desperately wanting to say yes to her offer, but how could I accept it? What would my friends think?

However, the thought of having a place to go and talk to someone who cared was a dream I longed to become a reality. So, eventually, I plucked up the courage and I went.

Those Thursdays quickly became the highlight of my week. Her office became an emotional filling station for me; it was a place where I felt connected, accepted and loved.

I realise, looking back, that this was the first time in my life that I had experienced unconditional love. Here was someone who was reaching out to me, not because of anything I had done *for* her, but rather in spite of what I had done *to* her.

She somehow knew just what I needed – it's the kind of insight that comes from taking a step back and asking, 'What is this child's behaviour telling me?' Rather than saying, 'look at what this child's behaviour is doing to me.'

It was this encounter that all these years later has led me to write this book. I wanted to look at managing behaviour from a different perspective, from a calm, detached place that enables a person to really understand where a child's behaviour stems from and how to help manage and improve it.

~

In her article, *'Building Resilience'*, social work consultant, Jo Fox, outlines a list of the key resilience factors for primary aged children and adolescents. The top resilience factor, that is, something that significantly increases a child's capacity to be able to cope in difficult situations is:

> 'The presence of an alternative, consistent, caring adult who can respond to the cognitive and emotional needs of the child.'
>
> (2010, p.13)

This alternative adult can be anyone in a child's life who makes that decision to invest: a friend, a relative or even a mentor or teacher. My form tutor became the consistent caring presence in my life as a pupil at my

London secondary school, which for me was the primary place where, through my behaviour, I sought to have my emotional needs met.

Even with the support of my form tutor, the change did not happen overnight because, as is well known, unlearning behaviour habits takes time. In spite of my continued disruptions, her commitment to me was relentless.

She spoke up for me: 'Tracey *is* capable, she *can* change.'

She stood up for me: 'I disagree with you, I think she has a wealth of potential, it just needs to be untapped.'

She stood by me: 'If you need me, I'm here.'

Throughout my schooling she was a constant source of encouragement, never ceasing to tell me what I could be. When I found myself on the brink of permanent exclusion she was there advocating on my behalf, promising her full support and commitment.

What stood out most for me at the time, was the fact that she looked beyond my behaviour. She didn't make allowances, but she showed an interest in the person behind the behaviour. She knew the names of my siblings, my favourite colour, my hobbies, my dreams and aspirations.

I remember the day she said to me, 'You have a smile that could light up a whole room.' What she did was to find a way to let me know that I was more than my behaviour and that, more than anything else, motivated me to change.

I can't stress enough how teachers can make a huge difference to children; we have so much power and influence over their lives. I believe we can use that more actively and positively.

~

I have met some amazing practitioners in my time, teachers who feel a real sense of calling to the profession and desire to make a genuine difference. The sound of laughter resonates from their classrooms, as the children respond to the creativity and vibrancy of their teacher. Their classrooms are bright, warm and inviting and the adults and children work in partnership under an agreed set of expectations.

For some, this picture may be somewhat idealist, but for many others this picture very much represents the way they work or at the very least the way they would like to work. If it were not for that one thing that they struggle to get a handle on: behaviour. This struggle is partly about the children, but it is so much more about us: our struggle to stay positive, to stay hopeful. Our struggle is to manage the strong feelings aroused in us because of challenging behaviour – feelings of despair as to what to do and how to move forward. Our struggle is to keep a child's behaviour separate from the person they really are, to like them even when we don't like what they do.

Three Stories

This book tells three stories and through them I hope to inspire you to be the One.

1. **My story:**
   A school girl who craved attention and was prepared to do whatever it took to maintain her position as top dog. A girl who feared no one, who challenged authority and who refused their every attempt to 'break her'. A girl who incurred six fixed-term exclusions, narrowly managing to escape permanent exclusion.
2. **A teacher's story:**
   My form tutor, whose care, compassion and commitment enabled me to get through my school years. A teacher who took the time to find out what my behaviour was really about. A teacher who refused to join her voice with the critics who said I wouldn't get past my negative attitude.

Instead of complaining about the 'darkness', this teacher chose to see my 'light'.

3. **Their story:**
The story of the countless children who I have worked with as a teacher and behaviour consultant. Children who are in desperate need for adults who will walk the walk and not just talk the talk. Adults who don't simply say, 'every child matters', but who also commit to ensuring that even the most challenging child in their class knows, beyond doubt, that in spite of their behaviour they too really matter. Children who in their own unique way, say to adults every day, 'Will You be the One?'

If you have the pleasure of working with children, the privilege of being a part of their daily lives, then I hope this book serves as a reminder as to why you chose 'them'. Remember, you chose children. You could have worked with animals, you could have worked in admin, but you chose children.

I hope this book informs you and builds your confidence as you face the daily challenges of working with children, particularly those for whom behaviour is an issue. Above all else, I pray it inspires you, reignites something inside of you that compels you to move beyond inspiration to application. That's where real change begins.

Amazingly, I am still in touch with my form tutor, my inspiration for both becoming a teacher and writing this book. In a recent conversation I asked her what made her invest in me the way she did back then. Here's what she said:

'Very early in your first year you did something I will never forget. At break one morning as I walked from our classroom you slipped your hand into mine and

walked down the corridor with me! In this moment I realised, among other things, how you, for whatever reason, had placed your trust in me. I could not destroy that. You might say I heard what you couldn't say. In your action you let me see your vulnerability; someone who needed protection and who was asking me for help and support. As a fairly decent human being what else could I do for you?'

I hold my hands up; I was a very challenging young girl, excluded from both primary and secondary school. My behaviour put me at real risk of being permanently excluded, certainly from secondary school. Astonishingly, I managed to defy the odds by not just becoming a teacher but an Advanced Skills Teacher in Behaviour Management. Imagine that, someone with my past now teaches teachers how to manage behaviour effectively. Now that's what you call ironic! However, I didn't do it alone and the truth is I may not have made it this far without a teacher who decided to be the One for me, to be there no matter what.

Ask yourself, 'Is there someone in my class who needs me?' Behaviour speaks and it says many things. I believe the young ones in our midst are simply saying, 'Will You be the One?'

My Philosophy

'Will You be the One?' was developed around what I believe to be key principles for managing challenging behaviour with an emphasis on teaching positive behaviour. At its heart is an unshakable belief that every child **really** matters and with the commitment and guidance of caring adults they can push beyond their perceived boundaries: they can grow, they can excel, they can achieve.

'Will You be the One?' is an appeal to adults involved in the education and care of children. It's an appeal for you to never lose sight of the child in the midst of their behaviour.

It's an appeal to always believe, always hope and always persevere.

This book is in two parts. The first is focused on inspiration and seeks to encourage you to hold fast to your original motivation for becoming a teacher. It is also hoped that it will serve as a timely reminder of just how significant our role is in shaping the lives of children.

Part two is about application and, having sought to put something into your hearts in part one, this section focuses on putting something into your hands. It outlines the key strategies and approaches needed to prevent and respond to challenging behaviour. It also provides instructions on how to build the kind of classroom environment that is encouraging and conducive to positive behaviour.

So here's a gentle reminder of what the teaching profession is really about...

PART ONE

Teaching: not league tables and levels, but lives

Why we really do what we do

I am certain that our reasons for entering the profession had everything to do with our desire to make a positive impact on a young life and nothing to do with an interest in school league tables. Part one of this book takes us back to the heart of teaching; the lives of the children we come into contact with and the opportunity we have to shape that little life for the better.

In this section I will share my own story and what I have come to understand about the reasons for my own childhood behaviour. You will also meet some of the children that I have had the pleasure of working with as I tell you their stories. As a behaviour management consultant I feel strongly about my obligation to put something into your hearts before I put something into your hands by way of strategies and tools. So, this first part of the book provides a number of opportunities for reflection upon our own practice because the management of behaviour is in fact cyclical. Children exhibit challenging behaviour and we adults respond to them. They in turn respond to us and so the cycle goes on. Our place within that cycle is vitally important, so I have explored in detail what behaviour is and how it makes us feel, as well as looking at what our behaviour and the behaviour of children is actually saying.

When someone leaves such a profound impression on your life as my form tutor did, it's no wonder I soon found myself wanting to do the same for the children in my care…

Chapter One

Could I do for them what she did for me?

The continuing effect of meeting the One

When an adult makes a decision to be a constant caring presence in the life of a child, the effects are far reaching. It can happen at any stage of your life. Call them 'the One' as I have, but what I'm really talking about is someone who cares enough to offer love and consistent support. The positive impact of that sort of unconditional love stays with you for life. I want to describe to you now, how the extra care and attention I received at school continued to impact my life and indeed the lives of both the adults and children I came into contact with.

It was in 2007, shortly after I had qualified as a teacher, when my passion for the area of behaviour management really came to the fore. I was invited to attend a Leadership Training Seminar along with some other colleagues from the school where I had been teaching. One of the sessions we attended was entitled 'Be a Change Champion'. Following a talk on the 'Toolkit for Change' we were set a task. We were given large sheets of plain paper and asked to draw a shield. We were then instructed to divide the shield into four and label each section. Two of the labels were: 'One thing I would like to change about my personal life' and 'One thing I would like to change at work'. I was sitting at a table with a number of colleagues from the London school where I was teaching: our headteacher, deputy headteacher, learning mentor, reception teacher and one of our teaching assistants.

As I busied myself filling out the four sections there was a lot of interest from my colleagues about what I had written in one of the quadrants. Under the label, 'One thing I would like to change at work', I wrote: 'People's attitudes to challenging children.' Those five words marked the start of something far bigger than I could ever have imagined. My colleagues pressed me for an explanation.

'Haven't you noticed the way some children are treated?' I began. 'Those children don't get a fair hearing because people assume that their reputation makes them guilty. The next time one of them is brought to your office, listen to the way that the incident is recounted. They are guilty until proven innocent. I think we could all do with some help about how to manage these pupils because it's not as simple as just having them removed from our classrooms. We need to be able to do more than just tolerate them, or simply punish them into submission.'

Like a torrent, my words just came gushing out. I knew it sounded a bit hard, but my comments were more about prevailing attitudes rather than a suggestion that I was right and everyone around me had it wrong. I felt discomforted by some of the interactions I saw between adults and children and wondered if there was more that we could be doing. I also sat there knowing full well the challenging pupil I used to be and the difference a caring teacher made to my own life.

The reaction of my colleagues was quite surprising as many of them began to share their own concerns about children and about our ability as a team to meet their needs and respond to their behaviour. We shared example after example of children for whom we had concerns, but ideas as to how to move forward were slow in coming.

The Challenge

Our headteacher waited until we were travelling back from the seminar before making a suggestion that caught me completely off guard.

As we cruised along the motorway she casually said, 'You need to deliver some training to the staff at school on behaviour management. I've watched you work with some of our most challenging children and they have flourished under your care. You have an amazing ability to remain positive even in the toughest situations. What you now need to think about is multiplicity. If you could transfer your skills to others on our staff team imagine how many children would be impacted?'

I was dumbfounded. What on earth did I know about behaviour management training? I was a Newly Qualified Teacher! At the time it felt like one of those moments where you wished that you had just kept your mouth shut. But before I knew it we were back at school and I was called into the office to schedule the date for the training. There was no turning back.

~

The headteacher in question, Dawn Ferdinand, is an amazing woman; a strong leader full of passion and vision. I had originally applied for a job as a Higher Level Teaching Assistant (HLTA) at the school and it was in the interview, after hearing me talk so passionately about my experiences working with children, that Dawn turned to me and asked, "Why are you not a teacher?" She let me know in no uncertain terms that if she were to give me the job, I would have to pursue a route into teaching.

From the start, Dawn conveyed such a belief in my ability and constantly placed me in positions where I could be challenged. Within weeks of joining the school as a HLTA, I was covering whole classes and by my second year, when my teacher training began, I was team teaching in a year six class, two thirds of whom were black boys who had a range of behavioural needs.

Dawn had watched me grow from a teaching assistant to a teacher and throughout that time I advocated very strongly on behalf of children for whom behaviour was an issue. Strong behaviour management skills, enthusiasm, and positive and caring approaches were consistently identified as strengths following my classroom observations. So in some ways it was only a matter of time before I would find myself further stretched under Dawn's leadership.

In preparation for delivering my behaviour training to staff, I was forced to look deep into my soul and ask myself some pertinent questions. *What is it you do? What do you do that enables you to relate so well and deal so effectively with challenging children?* The problem, however, was that I didn't know. I didn't know what I did, or at least I couldn't name it. That's the trouble with doing what comes instinctively, you just do it, you don't think about it. You don't worry about what it is called. You just know that when you do it, it works. How could I transfer what I could not articulate? I had hit a wall.

In addition, I had never taken part in any form of behaviour management training and therefore had no idea what this type of training comprised of. Along with this, the idea of standing before my colleagues, some of whom had been teaching for in excess of twenty years, filled me with fear.

Thankfully, two significant things happened which caused that wall of resistance to crumble. Firstly, as if someone had heard my cry, a timely circular arrived at school about behaviour management training taking place at the London Institute of Education. I could not believe the timing of it! It was a four day training course and fortunately the first day was just a few weeks before I was due to deliver my own training. Permission was granted for me to attend the training and when the day came I arrived at the Institute determined to have my thirst for knowledge quenched.

The training surpassed my expectations and I came away overflowing with knowledge and a better understanding of behaviour and how best to respond to it. One of the key things I came away with was an understanding of the strategies that, without even realising, I was already using. Being able to put a name to those approaches was crucial to me being able to transfer skills and ideas to colleagues.

The other thing that caused the wall to crumble was reflecting on my own schooling and the impact that my form tutor had on my life. I thought carefully about exactly what it was that she did to make me feel so hopeful that I could change.

I realised that my form tutor had communicated a real belief in me and I trusted her because her words were congruent with her actions. She didn't let me off the hook when it came to my behaviour, she was in fact very firm with me, but she didn't hold grudges – each day was a new day, affording me another opportunity to step closer to the person she believed I could be. As readily as she challenged and corrected me, she encouraged and motivated me too.

My form tutor defended me in the staffroom and challenged the prophets of doom who claimed to know what I would become. The challenge was how to apply this to the children in my care and how to encourage my colleagues to do likewise.

It was here that the realisation came to me; I needed to do for them what she had done for me. I decided in that moment that I would speak up for the children in my school in the same way that my teacher spoke up for me. My perception of the challenge set by my headteacher started to change and I began to view it as a unique opportunity to make the voices of the children heard.

I sensed the longing of the children for someone to be there for them, for someone to take a different view and a new approach with them. I wondered if we as adults talked less and listened more, what we might hear them say…

- 'Will you hold my hand and tell me that I can?'
- 'Will you say yes, when others say no?'
- 'Will you stay when others go?'
- 'Will you stand on the sidelines cheering my name, encouraging me to stay in the game?'

- 'Will you take the time to hear me out and speak to me without the need to shout?'

I decided that the training I was to give to staff needed to engage their hearts and cause them to think not only about the behaviour of the children but also about their own responses to it. I wanted to in some way be a voice for the voiceless; helping my colleagues to hear the children's perspective. I felt it was fitting to share my own story of multiple exclusions from school and the impact on my life of a single caring and committed teacher.

In essence, what I wanted to present to the team was a challenge: to do what we knew to be right and fair where behaviour management was concerned; **to turn common knowledge into common practice.** A challenge for us to hold on to hope and commit ourselves to an ethos that says, *'Every child matters. Every child deserves a chance. Every child can change.'* Having gathered my thoughts and pulled together what I considered to be the key principles of effective behaviour management, it was time to make my presentation to the team.

On 16th April 2007 I delivered my first behaviour management INSET entitled, 'Will You be the One?: Exploring challenging behaviour and our responses to it'. The reaction from my colleagues was amazing! They got it! Their feedback showed that they understood that what I was suggesting was nothing wildly new. It in fact reminded them of the original hopes and promises they held dear when they first came to the profession. Here are some of their comments:

- 'Moved and inspired.'
- 'Don't give up on any child.'
- 'Very powerful – lots of possibility and encouragement for reflection on our own practice and behaviour. EXCELLENT!'
- 'Food for thought – notice the positives and use the language of choice. Much needed inspiration.'

- 'I know you have made everybody feel that they have a lot to give the children – not an easy task! Well done!'
- 'Child centred, sharing own experience, linking to theory. AMAZING!'

There were tears too, as many of them heard my own story for the first time, and there was a heartfelt commitment to this new vision for behaviour management. What began as *my* philosophy for positive behaviour management quickly became *our* philosophy and I think it's fair to say that 'Will You be the One?' had been born.

The change in attitudes and approaches was almost instant; with people sharing good practice and asking for advice with difficult cases. There was a sense of positivity and commitment that permeated the entire staff team. What Dawn had said started to make sense: 'If you could transfer your skills to others on our staff team imagine how many children would be impacted?'

I had fanned the flames of that hope for the impact a teacher could make, and this had been my intention. Now, with this book, I hope to spread that impact further, of how we can truly make a lasting difference in the lives of the children who need our help the most.

That's what I live to do: **to touch the hearts of teachers and change the lives of children.** The fact that you are reading this book would suggest that perhaps you have that desire too. What step do you need to take to make that desire more of a reality?

Things to think about and do...

At the start of this chapter I described a task that I was asked to do while attending a training seminar. Completion of the task proved to be very significant for myself and the team I was working with. I have included a modified version of the task for you to complete in the hope that it will help you identify where change is needed within your practice and place of work.

One thing I would change about my responses to challenging behaviour:	One decision that I could make today to get started:
One thing I would like to change at my school:	One thing I can do to make this change possible:

Chapter **Two**

Can anyone hear me?

Listening to their words; discovering a window to their world

There are people you meet in this life who you never forget. For me, many of those people are little people: children. I consider it an immense privilege to have met and worked with the children I have come across in my life and work. Their stories have stayed with me and their faces are forever etched in my heart. In many ways it seems the right thing to do to share some of their stories with you.

Though I have not used their real names, the stories and events are real. Having heard them cry and witnessed their pain, I will share with you what they have told me as well as what I observed because you may also meet a child like them one day. I hope that as you hear their voices through these stories you will feel all the more compelled to listen to what children's words tell us about their world.

Daniel and Simone's stories below have been retold as if in their own words as these children were in upper Key Stage Two when I met them and therefore better able to articulate their feelings.

Daniel

'I just wanted something of my own. Everyone else had pocket money to buy stuff and I didn't have any. I didn't want to be the odd one out; I just wanted something of my own.'

My name is Daniel and I'm ten years old. I live at home with my mum, my stepdad and my little sister who's five. I'm in year six now and my teacher tells me that if I don't sort out my behaviour, I'm not going to survive at secondary school.

There are some things I like about school and some things I don't. I enjoy being with my friends and playing football, but I find reading and writing really hard. These days I seem to be getting into more and more trouble. Sometimes it's not my fault, but because I have been in trouble lots before, my teacher seems to think that it's always me who starts things.

My mum is getting fed up with having to come down to the school so often and my class teacher obviously doesn't like having me in class. I spend a lot of my time in other teachers' classrooms or outside in the corridor. I hate being in the corridor because when people go past they stare at me because they think they know why I'm there, but they never bother to ask me.

I was told yesterday that a mentor is coming to the school to help me. She's going to be working with me on my own to try and help me catch up with my reading and writing. Let's see how it goes...

The handover information I was given regarding Daniel was disturbing: numerous fixed-term exclusions, increasing aggression towards adults and children, little progress throughout Key Stage Two and minimal engagement from mum. The class teacher didn't have a single positive thing to say about Daniel and it was clear that his sessions with me were going to provide much needed respite for both the staff and Daniel.

Our first meeting back in 1995 is one that I will never forget. Daniel presented as a quiet boy, polite and very softly spoken. He was both sensitive and sensible and was acutely aware of how far he had fallen behind and how much his behaviour was affecting his learning. As I sat and listened to him I found myself waiting for the real Daniel to emerge – the one that I had been told about, the one that would swear and display physical aggression to adults. There was something about how he presented that just left me puzzled.

After a short while I stopped expecting the worst and I just accepted Daniel as I found him. It wasn't long before we built a rapport and as time went on, through subsequent meetings, I noticed more and more of a spring in his step.

I so hoped that it would continue. Little did I know that my work with Daniel would take many twists and turns, that there would come a time when the dam would burst and what would pour out would cause me such heartache and pain...

I knew Tracey really cared for me, I could just tell. I still got into trouble in class sometimes, but what I liked was that she always gave me time to explain. She asked questions and let me give the answers and if I said I didn't do it, or that it wasn't my fault, she believed me.

I don't know how she managed to convince my teacher to allow me to go on the class trip to the museum, but somehow she did. I was so excited I thought I was going to burst. My mum didn't remember to give me a packed lunch but it didn't matter because they gave me one when I got to school. This was a big chance for me to show everyone that I could behave and I especially wanted my teacher to have good news for my mentor when we got back.

I had barely stepped through the staffroom door the following Monday morning before I was hit with accounts of the 'shame and disgrace' Daniel had brought upon the school at the museum trip.

It emerged that Daniel had been caught trying to steal a rubber from the museum's souvenir shop. Consequently he'd not been allowed to come into school that day and it wasn't until a few days later that I had the opportunity to talk through the issue with him.

I remember the day well. I collected Daniel from his class as usual, but beyond hello, there was not another word uttered between us. I decided I would take him to the playground instead of the one-to-one room that I usually used. It was a sunny day and we sat across from one another on one of the picnic tables in the playground.

We both looked beyond one another and many moments passed before I began to relay to Daniel what I had heard. His posture spoke volumes – he sat with his head down and didn't say a word. I wasn't sure whether he would be willing or able to answer my next question, but I asked it anyway.

'Daniel, why did you do it?'

There was no response at first. Then suddenly he blurted it all out.

'I just wanted something of my own. Everyone else had pocket money to buy stuff and I didn't have any. I didn't want to be the odd one out; I just wanted something of my own. I took it because I didn't want people to laugh at me. I don't have anything of my own.' Each time he repeated 'my own', the more I could see him lose the fight to hold back his tears. Within seconds they streamed down his face and as the tears fell, so did the muzzle that had been on his mouth for years…

He went on to recount the years and years of physical abuse that he had suffered at the hands of his stepfather. The suffering that he had endured was harrowing and the more he spoke the more he seemed to want to say, as if he had been waiting a lifetime to tell his story.

The disclosure led to an investigation that culminated in Daniel being removed from his home and placed in the care of his biological father. I met his real father on a few occasions and each time he said very little, he would just grip my hand with both of his, look me in the eye and at the most say, 'thank you'.

This situation took place many years before I entered the teaching profession; I was barely twenty years old when I met Daniel, but I still remember it so clearly. I remember being young and inexperienced. I remember not always knowing what to do or say. But the year before, in 1994, I had gone to Camp America for three months and worked with inner city children and youths at a summer camp just outside New York City. It was a phenomenal, life changing time for me and I knew, from the minute I returned home, that I would spend the rest of my life working with children.

When I think about Daniel, I conclude that I was simply in the right place, at the right time.

~

Simone

'I used to have my mum all to myself, like to help with my homework and stuff. Now it's just different.'

My name's Simone and I'm eleven. For a long time it was just me and my mum and I'm not saying that we always got along but at least there was no one else in the way.

School is ok, I like it, but sometimes people get on my nerves. I get angry quickly and it's like I can't control it. I get into trouble a lot lately because of my anger.

My dad gets me angry as well, he says he's coming then he doesn't. Sometimes he lets me pack my bag and wait and then he doesn't show up. He doesn't get on with my mum but it's like he takes it out on me. I don't think that's fair. I can't really talk to my mum about it because she basically hates him, so with her it's just like she goes on and on.

I want to do better at school, but there's just a lot of stuff on my mind. Like my mum recently had my little brother and I'm not being horrible, but I just don't like him 'cos everything is different now. First of all my little brother's dad came to live with us and I didn't like that at all because it was just arguments all the time. Once, when he tried to hit my mum, I jumped on him and he threw me on the sofa. He doesn't live with us anymore but sometimes when we are out, we see him and he says stuff to try and scare us.

My teacher is nice, but I do mess about a lot in class. He says that it's like I am throwing my education away. I am bothered about that, but there are just times when I can't think. Like sometimes I'm in school and I'm wondering if my stepdad is following my mum around or calling her and saying stuff.

When I make my friends laugh in class that makes me happy. Every time I say something funny and they laugh, I wanna do it again and again.

My SATs are coming up soon and that's all everyone is talking about.

'You need to knuckle down Sims,' Mum says.

'It's going to be hard, but you can do it, you're more than able,' Mr Burns says.

I planned to do better, but my behaviour just got worse and worse and then one day I just exploded at my teacher.

'Why does my brother have to be around? I hate him! Before he came everything was fine. All he does is cry and cry all the time and my mum ain't got no time for me. She's always with him, patting him and rubbing him and even when we do get to spend time together, she's too tired. I used to have my mum all to myself, like to help with my homework and stuff. Now it's just different.'

I remember teaching a year four class and being alarmed at how many children openly talked about their disdain for their younger siblings. One child reported that he pushed his little sister down the stairs! Children often suppress these strong feelings because everyone around them is rejoicing at the new arrival.

When there is a sudden change in a child's behaviour try to be curious rather than angry. **They are putting on display what they cannot say.**

Mark

'I give sweets to people because I love them.'

I met Mark when he was six years old. Having completed my play therapy training, I was put on placement at the primary school where I met Mark.

Mark was living with his maternal grandparents owing to the physical abuse that he had suffered as a toddler at the hands of his father which had left him hospitalised for many months.

Mark was referred to us because his behaviour was becoming increasingly disruptive in class. He found it hard to stay focused on his learning and would run around and hide under tables. His grandparents had also been into school a number of times to report that his behaviour at home was also difficult, with Mark refusing to follow instructions and becoming aggressive. This behaviour came shortly after increased contact with his biological parents.

The playroom we used was filled with lots of different toys, instruments, puppets and games. There was also a big playhouse, sand, clay, water and lots of art resources. When Mark entered the room for his first session, he looked up at me as though awaiting instruction, then within seconds he was off, whizzing around the room like a tornado.

At one point he took out an instrument, started singing 'Twinkle Twinkle Little Star' then quickly broke off to ask me to read a book to him. I had barely read through the first page before he was off again; burying an instrument in the sand. He then played with some cups before burying them in the sand also. I watched him as he flitted from one thing to the next.

His play was quite competitive; if he hid something in the sand, I had to find it. When I pretended I couldn't find an object, he called me a 'silly loser'.

He also found it hard to follow instructions and I had to repeat myself a lot, particularly when it came to packing up time. Subsequent sessions followed the same pattern, with Mark whizzing in and whizzing around. During his play he would refer to characters as 'idiots' or 'silly billies' and, more often than not, he orchestrated play that involved him being in charge.

This pattern continued for a number of weeks. I was advised during supervision to sit in one place when Mark flitted around the room, as though to offer some kind of stability to him. I also set up a 'box for today' where Mark had to place all the items that he wished to play with during the session. It was shortly after making these adjustments with my position and the box that I noticed changes in him.

The first thing I noticed was Mark's grip on my hand as we walked from his classroom to the playroom; it became tighter and tighter as time went on. During the sessions he flitted less and talked more. He made a point of looking at me when he talked and his play became more cooperative.

'Do you want to be the shopkeeper while I make the sandwiches?' he said as we packed away the figures he had been playing with.

One day Mark took out a box of dolls and lined them up on the table. He sat back and looked at them.

'They look like a family,' he said. Then he took two figures from the 'family' and put them to one side.

'Is that nanny and granddad?' I asked.

'I don't call them nanny and granddad anymore,' he replied. 'I call them mum and dad. I have two mums and two dads.' With that he placed a doll – himself – in between nanny and granddad and put his mum and dad on either side of nanny and granddad. I rested my hand on the figures as we continued to talk about what he called 'family'. It was only when he raised his voice and said, 'Stop moving them!' that I realised I had inadvertently moved 'nanny' away from him.

As my work with Mark drew to an end, he became increasingly warm, gentle and softly spoken. He made a point of sitting very close to me during sessions and would often bring something into the room that he had made for me either at home or in class. I also noticed how he would make a point of saying my name as we talked and played together.

On one occasion, as we walked from Mark's classroom he said, 'I was looking for you this morning when I got to school, but I knew you were coming soon.' As we entered the room, Mark stretched out his hand towards me and as he opened it he slowly revealed a solitary cola bottle sweet lying in his palm.

'This is for you,' he said proudly, before skipping across the room to the toy cupboard, humming as he went.

'Is there anyone else you would like to give a sweet to?' I asked Mark as we tried on dressing-up costumes. There was no reply. 'What does it mean when you give people sweets?' I continued.

'I give sweets to people because I love them,' he eventually replied.

During our next session, Mark asked me to draw a bus while he drew one of the instruments. As we sat drawing, he said softly, 'This picture is for granddad. He lives with Maureen now because nanny told him to go.'

It's not always a happy ending and this is the sad reality of the work we do with children. We cannot whisk them away from their complicated worlds nor can we wave a wand and make everything ok. What we can do, however, is bring some stability. We can help these children make sense of the events in their world and more so their feelings about them.

Mark's behaviour spoke volumes about how out of control he felt. I don't know how much he remembered of his early experiences with his father, but he was clear about how he felt about them re-entering his life and where and with whom he felt safe.

~

Malcolm

'If I came straight into the room, I wouldn't feel comfortable.'

Malcolm was another child whom I met during my play therapy work. He was seven years old when we began working together and had been referred to the play therapy service because his teacher was concerned that he was becoming increasingly withdrawn. Malcolm would seldom speak in class and found peer relationships very difficult. His teacher stated that he appeared very preoccupied during lessons and at times seemed quite depressed.

During the sessions Malcolm didn't talk very much at first. When he did he spoke quietly and mainly about his little sister and mum. He appeared to carry a lot of concern for his mum and a lot of affection for his little sister. I learnt from Malcolm that his already overcrowded house had become even more cramped because of an older sibling returning to the family home. Malcolm was concerned that his mum wouldn't have enough money to feed the family.

'My mum has two jobs,' Malcolm explained, 'one that she does in the day and one that she goes to at night. Sometimes she gets back late in the mornings and I am late for school. I hate being late for school because everyone looks at me.'

He seldom talked about himself and sometimes, when I would attempt to make conversation, Malcolm would only shrug his shoulders. On other occasions he would begin to talk and then quickly cover his face and start to giggle. He was acutely aware of his mum's feelings and appeared to only be able to own emotions identical to hers.

It was interesting watching how Malcolm used the play space. He was very cautious and only played with a limited number of toys. He would also make a point of tidying away one toy before taking out another. This caution and hesitancy was evident from the minute he arrived. I would collect Malcolm from his class each week and we would walk side by side down the corridor to the playroom. What Malcolm did on entering the room was quite striking. I would open the door and walk in, but Malcolm would stand at the door and wait.

Each week I would say the same thing, 'Malcolm, I can see that you are standing at the door, when you are ready, you can come in.' After a short while he would enter, with shuffled feet and a look in his eyes that said, 'Really?'

My supervisor encouraged me to consider how overwhelming the space might be for Malcolm; a room all to himself, laden with toys and equipment – a place where he could just be, do and say whatever he wanted. I began to make the connections; the hesitancy, the tidiness, the thoughtfulness he showed towards me in ensuring that each week I too had something to play with.

'You can't just sit and do nothing,' he said once.

The playroom provided a kind of space that Malcolm had never known before. He showed me through our interactions, through his play and his drawings, how small and insignificant he was within his world. He had learnt to keep himself small and to keep himself quiet because he was so conscious of his mother's stress. He didn't seem to have a sense of self or a sense of identity beyond caring for his little sister and worrying about his mum.

It was at the start of our penultimate session that Malcolm announced, 'I'm moving today, did you know that?' I was so chuffed at Malcolm's news that I didn't anticipate what his drawing would soon reveal. He took a large piece of sugar paper and some black charcoal and began to draw his new flat. Once he had drawn the outline, he went on to colour the whole flat in black charcoal. I asked him how he felt about moving.

'I'm feeling bad about moving because there is no lift so my mum can't get the buggy down the stairs and my younger sister has a bigger room than me,' he said.

During our last session Malcolm drew another picture of his flat and again coloured it with black charcoal.

As he drew he said, 'I have to share a room with my little sister now because my older sister has come back from America and my other brother is moving back home.'

Interestingly, this last session with Malcolm was the only time that he walked straight into the room.

I once stood by him at the door and asked, 'What would happen if you came straight in?'

'If I came straight into the room, I wouldn't feel comfortable,' he said.

Children will use their behaviour, their work and their play to give us a window into their worlds. They use creative and often ingenious ways to speak to us, to call to us, to cry out to us. The idea is not for us to intrude, but to stand close enough, for long enough, so that we can *really* hear.

Things to think about and do...

- Even if things do not appear to be improving on the surface; persevere.

- When dealing with children whose home lives are difficult - focus on the things that are within your control, the things that you have the capacity to change.

Chapter Three

Behaviour speaks, so what does it say?

Behaviour roots and motives

Okay, we've had anecdotal evidence now let's have some research based theory to further deepen our understanding.

> 'It is impossible to understand a person correctly, unless one recognises the purpose of their behaviour.'
>
> (Dreikurs, 1977, in Tauber, 2007, p.148)

It is a widely accepted view that behaviour is the manifestation of unspoken feelings and the way we communicate our core needs. Both adults and children have a way of making their feelings known through their behaviour. Just imagine making a very special effort to prepare your partner's favourite meal and then having to watch them gulp it down with not even so much as a 'thank you'. It is highly likely that you or I would soon adopt some behaviours of our own that would make it known that we were hurt or upset by this behaviour. Or what about if someone barged into you in a queue and didn't say sorry? Would you not tut or roll your eyes in an attempt to communicate your annoyance?

In much the same way, children do not walk into class and say, 'I feel inadequate today,' instead they say, 'You can't tell me what to do!' as they toss their work onto the floor. For children, the idea that behaviour is a manifestation of unspoken feelings is significant and must be considered when thinking about effective behaviour management. While we adults may have the capacity to appropriate our behaviour responses, in many cases, children do not, and therefore, there is a pressing need for adults to seek to understand the feelings behind the behaviour.

Rudolf Dreikurs, the American psychiatrist and educator, said that, '...all behaviour - including misbehaviour - is orderly and purposeful and directed toward achieving social recognition... All misbehaviour is the result of a child's mistaken assumption about how to find a place and gain status. Parents and teachers need to be aware of what children do to be recognised and appreciated so that they can more fully accommodate them. They must also learn to avoid falling for the unconscious schemes children use to achieve their mistaken goals.'

(1968, in Edwards, 2008, p.98)

According to Dreikurs there are four misdirected goals of behaviour. Along with the motivation for these behaviours there is also a root cause as depicted in the table below:

Behaviour Motives	Behaviour Roots	What the child's behaviour is saying?
To seek attention	A fear of abandonment	"I only count if I'm being noticed or served."
To seek power/control	A need to feel significant	"I only count when I am in charge and I can make you do things for me."
To seek revenge	A need for justice for hurt caused	"I hurt, so you should hurt too."
To display inadequacy	A fear of failure and humiliation	"I can't do anything and I won't take the risk of asking for help. I need to convince everyone not to expect anything from me."

Attention Seeking Behaviour

Attention seeking behaviour is by far the most common goal of inappropriate behaviour, because children do not simply want attention, they need it. When this desire for attention goes unmet, children will quickly learn negative behaviour tactics to re-engage adults.

Let me begin by clarifying what is meant by the term 'fear of abandonment', because what I am not talking about here is a fear of literal abandonment, like being left in a car park or a shopping centre. I am referring to the kind of abandonment that a child could feel simply because their teacher is not standing close enough or is focusing his or her attention on other children. They have a fear that they will be overlooked and that adults do not have them in mind.

In reality we all have a need for positive attention from key people in our lives. However, for these children, particularly those for whom behaviour is an issue, it's a little more complex. By the time these children come to our schools they have already learnt, in most cases, that their poor behaviour brings attention from adults, albeit negative attention. Unfortunately, for many of these children, the only attention they get is when they are being addressed about their inappropriate behaviour because many adults, including parents, fail to appreciate the power and place of praise as a means of encouraging positive behaviour.

We overstate what we don't want them to do and understate what we do want them to do. We also underestimate how much attention children actually need and how hard they will work to get it. In her book *The Incredible Years*, Carolyn Webster-Stratton says:

> 'Simply stated... children will work for attention from others, especially parents, whether it is positive (praise) or negative (criticism) in nature. If they do not receive positive attention, then they will strive for negative attention since that is better than none at all.'
>
> (2005, p.18)

This statement is so powerful and important for us to hold in our minds as we work with children. Take a moment to reread it.

It's about giving our attention to the things that we want children to do more of, rather than the behaviour we wish to stop. More often than not we are not as quick to notice good behaviour as we are to notice poor behaviour and that needs to change.

Attention seeking behaviour can be:

- Calling or shouting out
- Incessant tapping or fidgeting
- Slouching or being lazy
- Talking loudly
- Whining
- Temper tantrums and children throwing themselves onto the floor
- Asking irrelevant questions
- Always needing extra help or claiming work is too hard

A child who seeks excessive amounts of attention from his or her teacher fast becomes an annoyance. These children only seem able to function when they have the approval of their teachers. I hate to admit it, but I was this kind of child: loud, always the one to do slightly more than what was asked. If the teacher said count to three, I would count to four. You know the type – yes, that was me. Let's go back to my story to look at these behaviours more closely and to shed some light on the underlying reasons for my displays of attention seeking behaviour.

The attention seeker in me

My story is by no means unique. Born to a father who had no interest in raising a child – quickly claiming I was not his – my memories of him are few: his insistence that I not call him dad and then at the age of ten being asked, 'Who are you?' when I naively called to him in the street one day. Now that I think of it 'Who are you?' was the last thing he ever said to me…

I am certain that my childhood behaviour was largely about my need for positive attention from key adults. Within my family I am the second child of five and our house was at times a very hectic place; where the undivided attention of an adult was a rarity. The father of my three younger siblings came into our lives when I was around four years old and as time went by I began to tell myself that I was not a part of the family picture that was being etched out in my home.

Children who seek attention have an underlying fear of abandonment and for me this feeling of abandonment was rooted in my dad's rejection of me and further compounded by my observations of the interactions between my younger siblings and their father.

My mum did a remarkable job with us and I can honestly say I have never met a more industrious woman. She went to the uttermost lengths to ensure that we had what we needed. Two things always strike me about my mother: her grit and her grace. From as far back as I can remember my mum had always worked hard and I'm not solely referring to her 'nine to five' job, but more so to the work she put in on our behalf. Looking back now, I'm not quite sure how she did it, but she did, relentlessly and selflessly. A woman of true courage and care.

My stepdad was a DJ and a very serious connoisseur when it came to soul music and I am certain that my love of music came from him. Music quickly became my refuge and I would sit and listen to my Walkman for hours, losing myself in the rhythm and the rhymes. Music shielded me from the elements like an umbrella in a storm. Like a warm duvet I would wrap myself in the melodies and the sounds and under the canopy of the harmonies my soul would find rest.

As is often the case with children who 'play up' at school, my behaviour at home was good and I pretty much just got on with what was asked and expected of me. At school however, it was a different story and it was in my latter years at primary school that my behaviour became a real issue for my teachers. I am quite boisterous by nature and when you couple that with a desperate need for attention it becomes hugely problematic. In class I would answer back, call out and create a song and a dance, all to get the attention of my teachers.

As I got older and became more and more aware of my popularity amongst my peers, the stakes became higher. I was now not only vying for the attention of my teachers but also fighting to maintain my position as top dog. I cherished my position as class clown, every joke, every prank, every showdown, affording me an opportunity to increase my popularity. I grabbed at those chances with both hands. It was no surprise then that by the time I got to secondary school, maintaining my reputation was my number one priority.

For some children, when they arrive at school, learning is not at the top of their list of priorities; relationships are the principle thing. I absolutely loved school and my attendance was good. At school I felt significant, it was a place where I belonged, where I found acceptance and companionship.

Looking back I feel incredibly grateful for the numerous friends that I had. They were completely unaware, I'm sure, of how much value they added to my life. Though I appeared to be the life and soul of the party, it was in fact my friends, my music and my sense of humour that enabled me to keep going.

One of my primary school reports says: 'Tracey likes to be the first and the best; she takes the slightest failure very hard... She is often cruel to other children, dealing out her own justice...' When I read through my old school reports now, they tend to make me wince and, if I'm honest, I feel a combination of regret and embarrassment at some of the things I got up to. On the other hand there have been times when I chuckle to myself as I picture my younger self refusing to go to the headteacher's office and then flip the coin and picture myself at the Institute of Education training teachers about positive behaviour management! **Truly, we do not know what children can become...**

Academically I always did well. In those days you left primary school as a band one, two or three. I left as a band one (the highest level), but I also left with one exclusion under my belt, having dealt out my 'own justice' on a classmate before school one morning.

By the time I arrived at secondary school, my 'mess ups' became more frequent. I had barely entered the second year (now known as year eight) when I incurred my first exclusion. After being told I was not allowed to take part in a netball match I proceeded to disrupt the whole game and refused to follow the P.E. teacher's instructions to go to the headteacher. What then ensued were a series of what I like to call 'spillages', where the feelings brought about by issues at home began to spill into my school life. At school I challenged my teachers in word and deed; every episode of defiance, every antic, filling a void.

With my reputation as top dog and class clown preceding me, I had to be seen to rise to every challenge; if anyone attempted to take me on, I had to take them out. There were spillages in the classrooms, spillages in the corridors and spillages in the playground. Teachers did their best with the clean up, but some did a far better job than others. Many of the teachers I encountered were far more interested in trying to 'break me', than they were in trying to understand me.

My form tutor was by far the best 'cleaner-upper' and the irony is that she probably saw the worst of my behaviour being both my R.E. teacher and my form tutor. Yet she believed in me the most. When she offered to sit and talk with me every Thursday after school, although I was slightly wary at first, it wasn't long before I began to treasure those times. Having the undivided attention of a significant adult was like water in a desert, like sunshine on a cloudy day.

What's important to state here is that there was no miraculous turnaround as a result of the input and care from my form tutor. It was in fact a good while before I began to settle down; before my need for attention began to dissipate against the backdrop of her constant care.

Many of my teachers referred to me as an attention seeker and I'm quite sure my form tutor saw me in much the same light. The difference, however, was that rather than looking for more creative ways to punish my behaviour, she sought to respond to the need. She somehow knew that I did not simply want attention, but that I needed it. My behaviour spoke to her and she took the time to listen to what it was saying.

Things to think about and do...

- Think of a child in your class who displays attention seeking behaviour. Are you taking time to find out what their behaviour is *really* about?
- What do you know about their lives that might explain their behaviour?
- What learning can you apply from this chapter to help to improve your relationship with this child and the impact of their behaviour on the class?

Chapter Four

What did you promise?

Remembering why you chose teaching

Advisory work was a huge part of my role as an Advanced Skills Teacher in Behaviour Management and I was often called upon to address a room full of teachers and school leaders. During training sessions I would often ask the question: 'Why did you come into teaching?' The answers were usually the same: 'to make a difference', 'because I like kids', 'to impart something of worth into a young life', and so on. All wonderful promises.

At the point of making these promises we had good intentions, but in the face of our daily reality it can be so easy to lose sight of the very reason why many of us entered the profession in the first instance. It's about children's lives; precious little lives full of potential and possibility.

So, again, what I'm advocating through my work and in this book is not necessarily a radically new approach but instead a simple reminder of what we already know. At regular intervals during our teaching career we all need to renew our commitment and remind ourselves of the core reasons why we came into teaching in the first place. As can happen in a marriage, the 'vows' we made on entry to the profession can get lost and forgotten, and a reminder such as this can help to re-orientate us and likewise provide a checkpoint against which to measure our progress.

Being a Promise Keeper

I remember being excited about the prospect of taking on a more senior teaching role in a new school. I had been at one school for many years and it felt like the right time to move on. I had always thoroughly enjoyed being a teacher and even in the midst of the mounting paperwork and numerous initiatives, aspects of the job that can really overwhelm you, I was always able to focus on the principle thing: the children.

During my first year in the new school it was easy to attribute the pressure that I felt to the fact that I had by far the most challenging class in the entire school as well as having to get to grips with working in a new environment with new processes and procedures. When I hit my second year, however, I couldn't understand why I still felt so weighed down by this sense of pressure and bewilderment. Though I enjoyed my time with the children, life in this new environment was proving to be quite a challenge. The team working in my class was amazing and there were some key members of staff that brightened up even the darkest day. In my heart, however, I carried a deep sense of dissatisfaction that began to weigh more and more heavily on me.

In the midst of the pressures and the politics, there was another 'p' that stood out for me: promises. It was during this season, more than ever before, that I had to remind myself about the promises I had made about the kind of teacher I would be. When it came to the children I had always promised the following:

- I would remain hopeful and positive.
- I would not make my issues their issues.
- I would be firm and fair, giving clear messages to the children.
- I would be there for them and that it was not their job to be there for me.
- I would be approachable, enthusiastic and consistent.
- I would be constant and reliable so that my pupils were never left wondering or worrying about what kind of mood I would be in.

Teaching is the kind of job where you need to be very 'present' and in order to ensure I could be available for the children I had to lean on my support networks like never before. I needed to be around people who would hear me out, but also keep me in line and keep me focused. In order to be child-centred – having the capacity to put their needs before our own; being able to pause, listen and respond rather than react – we need strong partnerships with colleagues or networks outside of school.

There are a number of things that have the potential to cause us to feel like the walls are caving in: from the behaviour of children or even adults, to the paperwork and politics. At these times we need to remind ourselves of the promises we made about how we wanted to practice.

It is at these moments that you need to engage in some positive 'self-talk', in order to remind yourself of what you said you would do and who you would be. It is very easy to get caught up in the day to day pressures of both looking after and looking out for children. It's vitally important that you have a way of reminding yourself of what you said you would do and also a way of measuring yourself against those standards.

What did you promise to yourself when you became a teacher? That you would make a difference? That you would believe the best of the children? That you would be non-judgmental? That you would not succumb to stereotypical views about social groups?

Different things will work for different people, but I have found the following advice really helpful in my attempts to remain present and focused as a teacher:

- **Maintain professional relationships with like-minded people.** This has been invaluable because we have been able to encourage one another and also hold one another to account.
- **Pin visual aids on the teacher's board in your classroom.** This has also been really helpful and a daily reminder of my priorities. For example, I wrote a poem called 'Will You be the One?' some time ago and there were moments when I would look up at it and allow the words to wash over me afresh. I have included the poem at the end of this book.

- **Keep children's 'thank you' notes and pictures.** As a teacher, particularly in primary education, you are inundated with pictures, notes of thanks and cards from children. I always used to keep a selection of them on my notice-board. There was something about the sweetness of their little pictures that reminded me of the place I held in their lives.
- **Know what you need and find a way to get it.** Everyone is different and what works for your colleagues may not work for you. Some people can keep going all day without a break or a snack. If that doesn't work for you, ensure that you get what you need to function at optimum level.

  If you work best when you have someone with whom you can talk things through, set up that kind of partnership with a colleague or line manager. I know some teachers who leave work at a reasonable time, but are happy to work in the evening at home. Then there are others who prefer to stay late and as a rule do not take their work home with them. What works for you? Know what you need and find a way to get it.
- **Don't be afraid to ask for help!** This sounds obvious, but often it's the obvious things that get missed. The issue with asking for help is that it calls for a level of honesty about how we are feeling. However, I'm sure you have heard it said that a problem shared is a problem halved! I have had the privilege of working in some amazing teams with people who made the journey so much more enjoyable.

  My teaching assistant (TA) for a number of years was a lady called Kim. After working with her during my first year as a teacher, I was adamant that whichever year group I found myself in, she was coming with me. Kim instinctively knew how to respond in a situation so as to ensure that I had appropriate support with the class. It was often something as seemingly insignificant as making sure I always had water to drink. As someone who suffers from headaches, drinking water throughout the day was really important. As a teacher often your needs are put on hold, so having someone alongside me who was not only in tune with the children but also in tune with me was a real blessing. These sorts of relationships take time to build and they work best when there is transparency and openness.

Our Powerful Position as Teachers

I remember reading the story of Rosa Parks to a year two class during Black History Month. The book began with Rosa Parks as a child sitting and listening to her own mother reading a story. I remember reading words to the affect of, '...as her mother read that story to her, she had no idea just who her daughter would grow up to be...'

I became really choked up because just below the book that I was holding there were a sea of faces staring up at me, hanging on to my every word. The reality of the powerful position I held as a teacher really hit me and tears filled my eyes. I had to push through to complete the book without the children wondering what on earth was happening to me!

As teachers we have no idea what the children under our care will grow up to be. All we know is that we have an opportunity right here, right now, to instil something that gives them a better chance at success than they had when we first met them. What a privilege! A golden opportunity that should be fully used and not wasted or worse, abused.

We have enormous power as teachers and I believe that the words of the late Dr Haim G. Ginott, written when he himself was a young teacher, make this point especially clear:

> 'I have come to a frightening conclusion. I am the decisive element in the classroom. It is my personal

> approach that creates the climate. It is my daily mood that makes the weather. As a teacher I possess tremendous power to make a child's life miserable or joyous. I can be a tool of torture or an instrument of inspiration. I can humiliate or humour, hurt or heal. In all situations it is my response that decides whether a crisis will be escalated or de-escalated, and a child humanized or de-humanized.'
>
> (1975, p.13)

The power that we hold as adults working in schools cannot be overstated. When the children cross the threshold into our classrooms – having been handed over by trusting parents who hope that we will treat them as if they were our own – we need to be careful how we handle our position and we need to remember what we promised.

Things to think about and do...

- What can you create that will serve as a reminder of the promises you made?
- How can you grow a network around you, so that you maintain the inner capacity to stay focused on the children?
- Reconsider your motivation for becoming a teacher. What are you now aware of?

Chapter **Five**

What's love got to do with it?

How your feelings affect your dealings

One of my all-time favourite films is *Freedom Writers*. Based on a true story, it charts the journey of Erin Gruwell in her first job as a freshman and sophomore English Teacher. Erin quickly learns that while she may have chosen the inner city high school for its integration programme, her colleagues believe that the integration programme has in fact ruined the previously A-listed school.

The staff do nothing to hide their disdain for the students and the classroom and resources allocated to Erin speak volumes about both the level of expectation and regard for the students in her class.

Though passionate and committed Erin is clearly unprepared for the lifestyles of the students she encounters, many of whom have strong gang affiliations and live according to a strict moral code of protecting their own at all costs.

Through unconventional methods Erin works hard to break down the walls of segregation between her and her students and indeed between the students themselves. She grows to love them and they grow to love her. Classroom 203 becomes a very special place for the students; a place they don't wish to leave, hence their heartfelt pleas for Erin to continue to teach them in their junior year.

It is from here that I would like to pick up the story; the point at which Erin goes into a meeting to negotiate teaching her class through their junior year. She knows she is not qualified to teach at junior level, but she makes her case anyway, knowing that the alternative is her colleague Brian Gelford, who regards the students as hopeless thugs. The tail end of the conversation between her line manager Margaret and Brian is very revealing:

Margaret: 'Believe it or not Mrs Gruwell there are other capable teachers in this school, if you have made the progress you say you have, your students should be ready

to move on. They might even gain something from more experienced teachers.'
Erin Gruwell: 'You can't teach them, you don't even like them.'
Brian Gelford: 'What has that got to do with teaching?'

I use this clip when delivering training in schools and there is usually a notable gasp at the suggestion that liking children has little or nothing to do with teaching. I ask participants to consider the following questions:

1. What does 'like' look like?
2. What does 'dislike' look like?
3. Does how we *feel* about children affect how we deal with children?

The responses are generally not surprising and there is usually a consensus around the idea that it would not make sense to work with children if you didn't like them. In addition to that it was felt that any dislike for children would soon be apparent in our interactions and behaviour. Participants also share their observations of interactions between adults and children where it is clear that the relationship is positive and a mutual fondness is evident. Conversely there were observations made of relationships where there was a level of dislike between the adult and the child and this too could be clearly seen.

The idea that a teacher, albeit in a film could ask 'what has liking children got to do with teaching?' is for many absurd. However, a little further reflection reveals that many adults in schools have in fact encountered situations where the dislike of a child or children has been very apparent. How we feel about children has a huge effect on how we deal with them and I'm sure we will all agree, when it comes to children whose behaviour is difficult to manage, the link between feelings and dealings becomes even more important.

Much of what we have already discussed has alluded quite strongly to our need as teachers to be intentional about our interactions with children. Here I would like to go a little deeper; to the heart of what I believe is the key ingredient needed to bring the kind of change that some of our children so desperately need.

Like Versus Love

According to the *Collins Dictionary*, to 'like' means to 'find agreeable or to enjoy.' The idea is that someone or something suits your taste. It also means to regard with favour or have a kindly or friendly feeling for a person or group.

When we start to think about what it really means to 'like' someone, we begin to see that actually it is somewhat unrealistic to suggest that in the context of our work with children we will like all of them all of the time. This, I'm sure is the case in any area of our lives as there are some people that we will meet to whom we may take an almost instant disliking.

There are other times when following a few encounters with individuals we may say, 'I really don't like that person.' The reasons for these feelings will vary; it can be as superficial as not liking the way someone looks or not liking someone's attitude or behaviour. We experience these feelings throughout our lives, in both personal and professional situations. Our prerogative to like or dislike people and things is a legitimate human reaction. However, it's what we do with like and dislike that really counts.

The reality is that some things will suit our taste while others will not. Some children we will like and other children we will struggle to like. 'Like' is fickle – it can be here today and gone tomorrow.

So, where does that leave us? Do we simply base our interactions with pupils on our feelings and allow them to dictate how we deal with children? Heaven forbid.

The question for me is not so much about like, but about love. Love, I believe, has got a lot to do with it. The kind of love I am referring to is not the fleeting 'here today, gone tomorrow' kind of love that we see on our television screens. The kind of love in question is what I like to call **love by volition, an act of the will, a decisive action.** It does not necessarily proceed from 'like'. It is very simply a decision to show warmth and kindness to an individual because that is deemed the right thing to do. It's the kind of decision we make regardless of how we feel. I heard a wise man once say, 'right feelings will follow right decisions.'

The children that we rub shoulders with day in and day out are at times not very likeable at all. That is why there is a need for something far more enduring than a mere liking. When it comes to children who exhibit challenging behaviour they need people in their lives who will say, 'I love you in spite of, not because of. I'm here for you regardless, despite what you do, because that is the decision I have made.'

The business of managing behaviour as we will see from further chapters is very emotive and strong feelings are exchanged between adult and child. It is imperative in the midst of these exchanges to be able to maintain a positive view of the child and hold in mind that they are in fact children who are on a journey towards more wholesome and socially acceptable behaviour. We also need to have made up our minds about how we are going to behave when we meet these children. Yes, that's right, how *we* are going to behave.

When children begin to lash out and challenge us in word and deed, we need something deep inside us that we can anchor on to. When you go into these situations having already decided to be the One, giving up is not an option, neither is getting even. When you enter into a situation with a made up mind to love unconditionally, you position yourself to be part of a lasting change in the life of a child.

It is from this standpoint that we can realistically still maintain a positive regard for a child who exhibits challenging behaviour. It is from here that we can chastise a child and then minutes later embrace them. It is love that enables us to do that. Love has got so much to do with it.

This is why I particularly enjoy training Post Graduate Certificate in Education (PGCE) students and Newly Qualified Teachers (NQTs) because this is the kind of decision they need to make before they even meet the children: **'Though your behaviour challenges me, I will still love you.'**

One NQT's story

I remember delivering a training session to a group of NQTs and, as was often the case, a number of them hung back at the end of the session to ask questions. I remember the look of despair on the face of the young teacher as she told me her problem.

She said, 'I've got a new boy in my class that I am really struggling to like. I was just beginning to feel as though I had my class settled when this new boy joined us. I find him really annoying and whiney. He calls out to get my attention and is struggling to make friends. I'm gutted because my class were really settled before he came and I'm conscious that I am beginning to feel resentful towards him.'

Her face grew redder and redder as she talked and I was sure she was going to burst into tears. I began by commending her honesty and acknowledged how difficult such an admission must have been. I went on to say that what she felt towards the boy was in some ways understandable in view of how far she had come with the class. I'm sure we can all appreciate how much of a significant step that must be when as an NQT you feel as though your class has finally settled.

I did encourage her, however, to think about what it must be like for him to come into a completely new situation and how desperate he must be to find a place to belong both with her and the class. I explained that it was likely that if she as the teacher felt that he had 'upset the mix' that the children probably felt that too and would no doubt let him know. Though I made it clear that her feelings were perfectly legitimate I did challenge her to consider what she needed to do in spite of what she felt. I also explained the pitfalls of allowing her emotions to dictate her actions.

Here lies a perfect example of a situation where a teacher needs to do the very thing that love commands; an exercise of the will in deliberate choice to do good, which does not necessarily run with the natural inclinations. This kind of love does not discriminate and is not reserved solely for those with whom there is some degree of affiliation. It is not self-seeking or self-pleasing; its object is others in whatever shape or size they come in.

I believe that this type of commitment and decisiveness can make a profound difference to the experience of children within our classrooms. I am calling for a level of self-denial that says although I have a right to feel how I feel, I am going to do what is right for the child. We are there for the children, they are not there for us; everything we do and say ought to be for their betterment. There is no room for passivity, for sitting back and waiting for feelings to change. We have to do what we know to be right and hope that our feelings catch up!

When negative feelings towards a child begin to surface, the adult needs to be proactive, to seek ways to improve the situation and indeed the relationship. It is easy to love when the going is good, **but it takes a special kind of person to love the seemingly unlovable, to teach**

the unteachable, and to choose to cherish children in challenging moments.

~

Some would argue that it is not appropriate to talk about love in the context of the work we do in schools. Personally I do not see how the topic of love does not feature. We do not work with machines, we work with 'little people' and in some cases these little ones are up against some big challenges.

Peter Imray, Special Educational Needs Consultant from Team Teach Ltd said, '...children do not have challenging behaviour because they want to; they are reacting to a particular set of circumstances at a particular time.' He went on to say that, 'the common features for most children who exhibit challenging behaviour is very low self-esteem and a poor sense of individuality. They therefore try to recreate themselves; their behaviour becomes their identity.'

(Team Teach Training, 3rd November 2010)

In the heat of the moment it is easy to lose sight of the fragility of these children.

One of the things that can help when we are easily overtaken with how we feel, is to try and remain child focused. By this I mean constantly asking ourselves what is going on for the child. When we accept the idea that behaviour is not random, that all behaviour is about something and is in fact a form of communication, we are better positioned to undertake the kind of reflection that brings a deeper understanding of the 'whys' of behaviour. He who knows why does far better than he who simply knows how.

It can be very difficult to engage in this kind of reflection when we view behaviour as personal – challenging behaviour is in fact seldom personal. Children by and large, do not sit down and dream up ways that they can antagonise their teachers. In many cases the behaviour is learnt and primarily about self-protection and preservation.

I would like to introduce Allan; a child I met a few years ago who very much epitomises the kind of child described by Peter Imray.

Allan's Story – Part One

While teaching a year five class, I became acutely aware very early on of the need for one boy to 'save face' when being challenged about his behaviour. I had earlier learnt that he had spent the previous two years becoming increasingly unmanageable: spitting, swearing, and absconding from class and school. Disruptions to lessons had become a daily occurrence. Upon hearing this report it was vital for me to consider just how important it would be for him in the face of a new teacher to prove to himself and his class that he still 'had it' so to speak.

I had to hold this in mind when dealing with his behaviour because the boy in question would often want the last word, feeling the need to turn something minor into something major. For him the boost to his self-esteem that he gained from his defiance was far more potent than the threat of a consequence. So it was important for me not to get drawn into verbal 'ping pong' matches and to make sure that I tactically ignored what I could and kept the emotional content low for the things that could not be ignored and had to be dealt with.

Allan was a classic attention and power seeker. There were two significant themes about his school life before my arrival that were of particular interest to me. Firstly, the two years that I referred to earlier were not spent in the driver's seat; Allan was a passenger, he was very much an 'I'll come along for the ride' kind of child. He was not a leader, but a follower. Secondly, the leader of the pack, a boy previously in his class, had moved on from the school just before my arrival, which meant that Allan was now on his own. Without 'Batman' what would Robin do? Who was he to be without someone leading, suggesting and goading?

These are the things I considered when I thought about the prospect of being Allan's teacher. I knew that he would be desperately trying to maintain and protect his image as the non-compliant one and that would be a tall order for him without his 'puppet master'.

These reflections in some ways prepared me for the battle that ensued. It certainly helped to have given thought to how he would be feeling rather than being preoccupied with my own feelings about the prospect of teaching him. As I do when faced with a request to work with difficult children, I relished the challenge and, more to the point, the opportunity to make a difference.

The need to build a trusting relationship with Allan was paramount and it was essential to make it very clear to him that I wanted him around. The rest of the class also needed to accept that despite his challenging behaviour Allan was a part of the class and needed to be regarded as such. So during those early stages I worked hard to communicate my commitment to him and, though I made it clear that I would not compromise on the teaching and learning, I likewise emphasised my desire to help him make the necessary adjustments to be a part of our class.

It was by no means easy and there were days when I had to dig deep to find just a little bit more patience to deal with him. During the first three months Allan continued to test boundaries and when challenged he would simply leave the room. It didn't help that he was habitually late most mornings and what he presented on entry was a combination of uncertainty as to what to do and difficultly self-motivating.

As Allan struggled to make the transition, the response from his classmates was interesting to observe. He didn't get the rise from them that he was accustomed to; they were no longer interested in his antics. The boundaries in class were firm and expectations high and it was clear that the class had bought-in to the way in which we had agreed to work together. Allan simply didn't have enough influence to sway them. He was out on a limb, struggling to find a way to relate to his peers outside of his disruptive behaviour.

It soon emerged that underneath his bravado was a feeling of insecurity and I wanted to leave him in no doubt that while he may have felt unsure of his classmates, he had no need to be unsure of me. I made certain I had a place I could channel my frustrations, so that in my dealings with him I could constantly hold in mind what was going on for him, rather than be overshadowed by my own feelings.

Children who habitually exhibit challenging behaviour are often the victims of repeated rejections within their relationships both inside and outside of school. People decide very early on that they have had enough and children get the message that they have had enough of 'them' rather than their behaviour. In some cases these children decide to get in there first by rejecting adults and so save themselves having to deal with the heartache of being rejected later. They get so accustomed to adults not going the distance with them that it can take a long time for them to develop the trust necessary to build lasting relationships.

Allan would have known that I had received a handover from his previous teacher. He may or may not have considered what I thought of him or expected of him in view of what I had heard. The information gleaned from a handover or from a child's file is no doubt helpful in some ways, but teachers have to be very careful not to allow what they read or hear to cloud their judgment or limit their belief in a child.

Regardless of what I had heard about him, the boy who stood before me was scared, he was insecure. He was stuck in between who he used to be and who he could become. As his teacher, I had a responsibility to take him as I found him and to make a commitment not to leave him that way. As you will hear a little later when I pick up Allan's story again, his behaviour evoked some very strong feelings in me and I can honestly say I had some of my most challenging encounters as a teacher with him. There was, however, something deep in my core that would not allow me to lose sight of him in the midst of his behaviour.

Shortly after I left the school I saw Allan in a local park with some other children from his class. By this time he was at the tail end of his primary education. As I stood chatting with some of the other children from his class, he came over and simply said, 'You see Miss, I made it.'

What's love got to do with it? A whole heap.

Things to think about and do...

- What is the difficult decision that you are avoiding?
- Have you been waiting to 'feel right' about it before making it?
- Remember right feelings follow right decisions; they don't always precede them.

PART TWO

From inspiration to application

Something in your hands, now that you have something in your hearts

Part one was about inspiration and brought us right back to the heart of teaching; the children. We looked at how the 'Will You be the One?' philosophy was birthed before hearing from the children themselves and learning about how they manifest their core needs through their behaviour. Having considered our own responsibility to ensure that we have the support and tools to manage the strong feelings that can arise from dealing with challenging behaviour, it is now time to move on to part two of the book.

I have approached the writing of this book in the same way that I approach my work and in particular my behaviour management training sessions; by ensuring I have deposited something into your hearts before putting something into your hands. Being comes before doing and with that in mind I have sought to encourage you to reflect on **who** you are before giving you advice on **what** to do.

I am steadfast in my belief that it is from this premise that we can really begin to make maximum impact; remembering that children's behaviour is not directed **at** us as much as it is communicating **to** us. Having taken the time to pause and remind ourselves about the promises we made, let us now move on to the more practical aspects of behaviour management: from inspiration to application.

In part two we will look at the key elements of effective behaviour management. The key word here is 'effective'. You see, anyone can 'manage' behaviour; particularly when you are dealing with young ones like we do. A raised voice and a stern look will suffice for many of our children, but effective behaviour management is where some degree of learning happens and a child comes away from a situation with a clear idea about what they have done wrong, why it was wrong, and what they need to do differently next time.

We are going to begin with a look at communication because it is such a key component to effective behaviour management, as many of our strategies require oral communication with children.

So, get your toolkits ready for the first deposit; some ideas about how to speak so that children hear and heed!

Chapter Six

You said it, but did they hear you?

The real deal about communication

In this chapter I'd like to consider how we communicate with children, why it sometimes goes wrong and what we can do to ensure we get the desired outcomes from our communication with them.

> 'A wise teacher talks to children the way he does to visitors at his home. If his guest, Mrs Smith, forgot her umbrella, he would not run after her shouting, "Scatterbrain! Every time you visit my home you forget something. If it's not one thing, it's another. You'd probably forget your head if it weren't attached to your shoulders. I want to live to see the day when you remember to be responsible for your own possessions. I am not your slave to pick up after you." His comment would probably be, "Mrs Smith, here is your umbrella." Yet the same teacher feels almost compelled to criticise a child who forgot his books or lunchbox or glasses.'
>
> (Ginott, 1975, p.84-85)

You may or may not have seen this sort of behaviour first hand – adults who have a very different way of communicating with children compared with how they communicate with adults. In some cases, as can be seen in the example above, the difference is startling.

Within schools, it has already been established what we will do in response to behaviour incidents because it is the behaviour policy that sets out the agreed protocol, but how we do it is down to us. This is where things can get a bit messy - in the communication stage.

The 80s pop group Bananarama had a song entitled, 'It Ain't What You Do (It's the Way That You Do It).' When it comes to effectively communicating what you want in the classroom, I would say, 'it ain't what you say, it's the way that you say it, that's what gets results.'

The result that we are looking for when communicating with a child about their behaviour is an understanding of what went wrong and an idea of how to do it differently next time. It's all about learning!

Unfortunately, what often happens in schools, as well as at home, is that the response to behaviour is so emotionally charged that the opportunity for learning is missed. The only thing that has been noticed by the child is the emotion on the part of the adult.

> 'When you are emotionally charged people catch your emotion but miss your point. We are responsible for how we deal with what we feel.'
>
> (Desmond Brown, Leadership.com, 6th May 2012)

When measuring the effectiveness of communication we are aiming for the message to be accurately passed from the sender to the receiver. In order to achieve this we need to broaden our understanding of what constitutes effective communication. The chart below is a representation of the research findings of Mehrabian & Ferris, 1967, as stated in the *'Journal of Consulting Psychology'* p.248-252. When it comes to communication, actions indeed speak louder

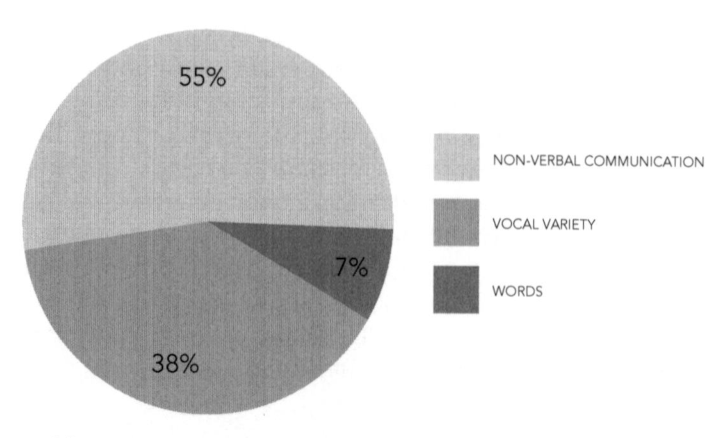

than words. It is not so much what you say, but what is **seen** and **felt** that counts.

This chart shows the actual amount of information picked up by the receiver during any form of verbal communication. You will notice that the smallest amount of information received comes from the actual words spoken.

Non-verbal communication
This refers to expressions, posture and gestures.

Vocal variety
This is about tonality, including both tempo (how fast or slow you are speaking) as well as timbre (which is the texture of your voice, be it rough or smooth). All of these things affect the quality of the message we give to the receiver.

It is no surprise then that only 7% of what is picked up by the receiver relates to the actual words spoken. So if we were to re-order this chart in simple terms we would say: It is what you look like, how you sound and then what you say. You only need to watch a mime act to appreciate the power of non-verbal communication.

> '...when a person's words disagree with what is conveyed via his tone of voice, gesture, or other nonverbal channel, the emotional truth is in how he says something rather than in what he says.'
>
> (Goleman, 1996, p.97)

People will always notice how you say what you say, before they catch what you actually said. So be careful what you throw out.

In the context of our work then, it is worth giving some consideration to how we communicate with children – how we can speak so that they can hear. The best way to achieve this is to make certain there is congruence between what you are saying and how you are saying it.

Congruence is achieved when all the communication channels outlined in the diagram are in alignment. For example, my words to a child are, 'Well done, you remembered to use capital letters for names.' I say them with a smile on my face, while giving the child a 'thumbs up'. Both my verbal and non-verbal communication is congruent, which makes it more believable and increases the likelihood of the message being received.

One of the first strategies I mentioned earlier was about staying calm and while I appreciate this is much easier said than done, the reality is that we have far more chance of being heard when we are calm. I constantly remind myself and those I train to **keep the emotional content low, so you can stay in control.**

Here are some key ingredients for good communication:

Say it like you mean it

Does your tone match your talk? When giving praise to children you need to ensure that your tone sounds bright. It may even help to put a smile on your face! Think about what other gestures you could use to reinforce the message – maybe a thumbs up, a high five or a wink.

Conversely, when giving a correction, an assertive tone is needed to communicate that what is being said is non-negotiable. Everything about your tone and your body language needs to indicate that you are clear and in total control. Being assertive is very different to being aggressive. Aggression is about control through fear – it's reactive and hostile and more often than not breeds the same type of response from children. Being assertive is about being clear about your expectations and communicating this in a measured and controlled way. An assertive adult is sure of themselves and their ability to handle a situation.

Let me add here that contrary to popular opinion, both shouting and whining indicate a loss of control. Whining sounds powerless and feeble and can give children the impression that you have lost the battle or in fact the will to fight. Shouting should only be used where a child's safety is at risk. In any case, if your first response to misbehaviour is to shout and the child does not comply, what will you do next? In these situations teachers can feel embarrassed as a result of raising their voice and still not getting the desired outcome. This can lead to the teacher shouting even louder and becoming embroiled in a power struggle with a child.

The other issue is that children who habitually exhibit challenging behaviour would have certainly been shouted at many times both at home and at school. So if shouting was going to work it would have done so already. As these children are very accustomed to being shouted at it does not cause the sense of alarm that it might arouse in a different child. In fact they actually block it out, as if to say, 'I've heard all that before.' This subsequently arouses further anger and frustration on the part of the adult.

Tell them, don't ask them

'Could you stop please?', 'Would you like to go to timeout?' or 'Why are you making that noise?' These are all irrelevant questions when it comes to effective communication because we in fact do not want an answer to any of these questions; we just want the negative behaviour to stop.

Can you imagine if following the question, 'Why are you making that noise?', a child turned around and said, 'I'm keeping myself entertained because your lesson is boring!' We would be mortified! We do, however, waste a lot of time asking questions when we should be giving instructions. Try to resist the urge to begin a sentence with 'could you', 'would you' or 'can you'.

Instead, rephrase the questions: 'Please stop what you are doing', 'Please go to timeout' or 'Please stop making that noise.' These are clear instructions that leave no room for ambiguity or negotiation.

Be descriptive about what you want to see
What do you mean when you say 'sit nicely' or 'play nicely?' Try to be more descriptive by saying, 'I need to see you looking this way with your arms folded', or 'I would like to see you sharing the toys and speaking to one another in a calm voice.' It's clear and it's descriptive. When it comes to young children they need to be told what to do with their body parts – 'Eyes this way, legs crossed and hands in your laps.' If you don't tell them what to do, they will decide for themselves!

Be aware of the impression you make on children
What I am talking about here is presence; what you bring with you when you walk into a room. You will have met people who have a calming presence and others whose presence creates a sense of anxiety and uncertainty. What I am asking you to consider in essence is **what is it children get when they get you?** Think about the following questions:

- What kind of presence do you carry?
- Do you come across as being warm and approachable or cold and hostile?
- Do you have a stern face or is it friendly?
- What does your natural voice sound like? Is it high pitched? Is it squeaky? Does it sound harsh? Does it have an edge to it?

I have a strong presence and naturally assertive tone, but I use a lot of humour when I am teaching. I find that the balance between my tone and use of humour helps to create a relaxed atmosphere in my classroom. Children know that we can have a joke and a laugh, but they are likewise very clear where the boundary lines are.

Timing

The principle thing when dealing with an emotionally charged child is to help them to calm down. It is not the time to give them a lecture or to meet them with equal emotion: anger + anger = more anger!

Instead allow time for them to calm down so that they are in a better position to hear what you are saying. Also consider how hard it can be to take a correction or a telling off with good grace; be careful not to get taken up with secondary behaviours to do with posture and eye contact. The body language of the child is going to reflect the fact that they are being told off, allow them the space and time to express that appropriately.

Remember to stick to the matter at hand and don't be tempted to take the opportunity to remind the child how many other times you have had to talk to them about the same issue. I will never forget what a year five child once said. When asked what 'hots things up' in a conflict situation she said 'talking about the past when it is a present problem.' I shall say no more!

Children also appreciate warnings about things, rather than things happening suddenly. For example, if children are playing and pack away time is approaching, give a time warning so that they know that the end is nigh. Allow children time to respond to what you have asked – don't turn things into a stand-off. State what you expect and then move away because this communicates that you have faith that they will do what you have asked.

Repetition
When it comes to children, once is seldom enough – be prepared to repeat yourself. Also consider how you can make instructions sound more fun: 'Who is going to be the first one to clear away the toys?' Again, think about your tone here; children will not interpret an instruction as fun if you sound agitated.

Passive, Aggressive and Assertive Communication
There are typically three types of communicators: passive, aggressive and assertive. Whatever your natural approach is, it is important to understand the impact of these approaches in communications with children. Each style of communicator has a distinct sound that is amplified by the gestures and body language that go along with the chosen approach. While some people may consider themselves to be naturally passive or aggressive, it is vital that within your toolkit you have a range of ways of communicating with children; tools that can be summoned up and used depending upon what you are trying to achieve.

Passive
In the context of teaching, passive teachers are generally vague and unclear. They lack the confidence to confront problems and only enforce some of the rules some of the time. Pupils quickly become lost and unclear about what is expected and they begin to take control and advantage of such situations.

Picture this scene: a group of reception class boys are playing with cars and there is the sound of crashing, banging and sirens. In the midst of that the teacher says in a soft whimper, 'Boys put your toys away please.' Are they really going to take that request seriously? Will they even hear it? Did the tone communicate that there would be consequences for non-compliance?

Aggressive
On the other hand the aggressive teacher rules through fear. It is very much a 'do as I say or else' approach. Children will generally comply to begin with, but there is often a level of resentment and after a while children lose the feeling of fear and begin to match the hostility shown to them. Children do not know where they are because aggressive teachers tend to be quite reactive. They fly off the handle and lose control very easily. Contrary to their beliefs about themselves and their level of authority, it is usually frightfully obvious to children that control has been lost. As I said, there is initially a level of compliance from children, but little relationship or respect.

Assertive
The assertive teacher is calm, clear and controlled. They know what they want and they make their expectations clear. These types of people are firm and fair. They act rationally rather than allowing their emotions to dictate their responses and because of this sense of control the way they communicate builds the esteem of children. Children feel safe and secure in these situations because they know what is expected and their positive relationship with the adult helps them to recover well from setbacks.

Clearly this assertive approach is the one to aim for; where emotions are kept in check and all parties are clear about what is expected. The suggestion is not to try to become a different person but to adopt the approaches that are most suited to the situation that you find yourself in.

Much of our practice as teachers involves the art of effective communication, but when it comes to behaviour – where logical thinking can be hijacked by powerful emotions – it is vital that we keep a handle on both what we say and how we say it.

Things to think about and do...

- Is there someone who can give you some objective and specific feedback about how you come across to children?

- The reality is that some people are better at assertive communication than others. The key thing is to identify your strengths and commit to developing the weaker aspects of your communication skills.

Chapter **Seven**

Can't you see, you are expecting too much of me?

The importance of letting children be children

Let us begin with a definition, again from the *Collins Dictionary*:

- *ex-pec-ta-tion*

1. The act or state of expecting

The word suggests that an individual holds a strong belief that something will happen, so much so, that they anticipate it.

Fundamentally, expectation is what we have chosen to believe and expect from a child. The reality – whether it be in a classroom or a living room – is that what we believe shapes our behaviour. That is why I pay far more attention to what people do than to what they say; in fact what we both do and say is born out of what we believe in our hearts. We know all the buzz phrases very well 'every child matters', 'I have a duty of care', 'I came into teaching because I care about children', the list goes on and on…

However, what you really believe is manifested in what you actually do on a day by day basis. In writing this book, one of my objectives is to show how these fundamentals of good teaching need to shift from common knowledge to common practice.

A few questions for us to consider:

- Why is it that some children are placed on the special needs register at age five and are still on it at age ten? Could this be about expectations?
- Why is it that a child can be in the lower ability group in school for the whole of their school life? Could this also be about expectations?

Yes, there will always be complex reasons why children do not achieve and excel at the same rate as their peers, but I'm not convinced that it is always that complicated. As teachers we sometimes lose sight of our responsibility to be gatekeepers; creating access points for all children to discover and realise their full potential.

The pressures of the classroom can make it hard to differentiate appropriately and while we are skilled at giving children work that they can access, we sometimes fail to give them enough exposure to work that could challenge, extend and stretch them. It would seem that inadvertently we have placed children in a box and that is where they tend to stay, and when we hand over our class to the next teacher we hand over our low expectations and so the cycle continues.

It is important for us to consider expectations from two angles: those that we have of children who are well-adjusted and those that we have of children who are vulnerable and challenging. It is important to acknowledge that these children start from different baselines and therefore what may be achievable for one child, may take a little longer to develop in another. The key is for us to meet children where they are, but not to leave them there.

For example, when I first met Allan (who I introduced in chapter five), I was informed that he generally did not stay in class for more than fifteen minutes before absconding. So when I began teaching him I did not insist that he stayed in class all day, every day because he hadn't been able to achieve that in over a year. What I did was celebrate his efforts in trying to extend the time he spent focused on a task in class, before gradually increasing my expectations. I took him as I found him, but I did not leave him there.

While delivering an INSET in an East London school, I asked the participants (with reference to the children), 'Does their deprivation affect your expectations?'

I went on to explain that children do not need us to feel sorry for them. The facts and statistics about deprivation, poverty, single parent families, and alcohol and drug abuse are what they are, but it is what we choose to believe about each individual child that really counts.

For some children the adults around them have fixed ideas about who they are and in fact who they are going to be. The power of belief is still one of the most important resilience factors a child can possess. The presence of a significant adult who believes in them can change a child's life forever.

Sometimes children's behaviour is misdiagnosed as being challenging when in fact their behaviour is perfectly acceptable and appropriate for their age and stage of development. This is why a child-centred approach to both teaching and parenting is so vital to our relationships and our work, because it helps us to be fair with the expectations we place on children.

They will be excitable because they are children. They will be inquisitive because they are children. They will become restless because they are children. How much room do we give to children to just be children?

Expectations – Keeping it Real

It is often said that you shouldn't take your personal life to work, but teachers are still people who have both personal and professional lives. When I have experiences in my personal life, be they positive or negative, they have an effect on me and it is the same 'me' that I take into work on a Monday morning. I cannot cut away the part of me that has been adversely affected by circumstances and take the rest of me into work. When we arrive at our places of work, we take our whole selves into that space.

The issue is not whether we take our personal lives to work – I'm not convinced we have a choice in that – but about how we manage the feelings brought about by life's issues while at work and, in particular, in our work and interactions with children. It helps to remind ourselves that we are very much like children – we are just bigger and more experienced. If we were to stop and consider the things that make us tick and the things that tick us off in terms of human interactions, we would take a significant step forward in our understanding of children.

As an adult I do not like it when people don't keep their word, I don't like people shouting in my face and I don't like to be misunderstood and misinterpreted. On the other hand I like it when people show faith in my ability, when people are fair and consistent with me, and I like it when people consider my feelings. This is by no means an exhaustive list, but I'm sure you get the point.

Here's another thing… As an adult I need to have a place where I can take my 'stuff' – when things get a little too hard to bear. I need to have people around me that I can talk to, to share with and to offload. Wayne Cordeiro of New Hope Christian Fellowship referred to these people as 'lightening rods' – people that we can go to and talk things through with, so that innocent people aren't burnt by the 'fire' that we carry.

As adults, at home or within a school, we are constantly self-regulating to ensure that we can give the best of ourselves to the children within our care. If we as adults with a degree of maturity and professionalism feel the need to push against the pressures of life to ensure we stay grounded and focused, how much more so are the young ones needing to do this?

Educators have long recognised that a child is a whole child and that how a child feels and acts is inseparable from how they learn. The 'SEAL Programme' (Social and Emotional Aspects of Learning) now widely taught in schools is a response to the government's recognition that if children are anxious, angry and depressed they cannot learn. Children now have more and more opportunities in school to learn about why they feel what they feel and how these feelings affect them and their relationships. They are also taught coping strategies and how to engage in peaceful problem solving.

Often the expectations we have of children can be far too high. We sometimes overestimate their ability to cope and to carry loads.

I'm Too Small to Carry That

You may have noticed that in some parts of this book I make reference to the home and parenting, this is because as part of my work as a behaviour consultant teacher I also work with parents, helping them to establish the kind of home environment that is conducive to positive behaviour. The programme for parents is called 'Behaviour Basics' and during this I talk about children starting the day the right way. I say to parents, 'The only thing children should have on their backs when they arrive at school is a rucksack with the appropriate equipment needed to fully engage in all that the school day has to offer.'

However, as we well know, all too often children arrive at school heavy laden – their 'rucksacks' full of things they should not have to carry. Examples of these burdens are:

Anxiety

- 'Who is picking me up today?'
- 'How come daddy didn't come home last night?'
- 'Why was mummy crying?'
- 'I wonder if mummy and daddy are still arguing?'

Fear

- 'What was that fighting on the news last night?'
- 'I'm going to get told off for not doing my homework and there's no point telling my teacher what was happening at home because he won't believe me.'
- 'My friends are going to laugh at the hole in my trousers.'

Fatigue

- 'I have so much to do before I leave for school that by the time I get here I'm really tired.'
- 'I was up until late playing on my Xbox.'
- 'During the night my brother came home and when he came into the room it woke me up.'

Some children arrive at school in such an emotionally stressed state: hyper-vigilant or withdrawn, inattentive or preoccupied. For many of these children the last thing on their minds is learning. Often they are tired and hungry; having not had breakfast or enough sleep. In other cases children have simply been overexposed to adult issues and arrive at school mentally flooded and unable to actively engage in learning. Many children who have difficulty managing their behaviour are dealing with far more than we can see and for some their behaviour is in fact more a cry for help than a protest.

As teachers we need to consider how we support children whose life circumstances make them vulnerable. In times past I have set up a 'check in' system for the vulnerable children in my class. It was a simple process whereby the child / children in question would check in with me or a teaching assistant on entry to school in the morning. This was usually through the use of feelings vocabulary or illustrations whereby the child would simply come into the class and move their name to the word or illustration that best described how they were feeling. This system gave us a 'heads up' as to the frame of mind that child was in on entry to school and it also allowed them to have their feelings acknowledged by an adult without having to explicitly express them.

Another factor is that some children can be 'under-developed and overexposed' to adult issues. As adults, we need to monitor how much we allow our children to see and hear, not just on the television but in our conversations.

Children should not be the ones with whom we share our frustrations about the other parent; adult issues should remain amongst adults.

I'm Only a Child – Let Me Be

One thing we can be sure of is that children will be children and as adults we need to be clear that our expectations take that into account. One of a number of disheartening situations for me is that of a child who is not permitted to be a child; a child who is inhibited by over-anxious adults, who is not permitted to laugh or cry, who is berated for asking too many questions or for being too excitable or energetic. Children need to be given permission to appropriately express themselves: whether it be an expression of joy or sadness. Our job is to help children understand that there is an appropriate way, time and place to express these feelings. Alongside this, children need to be given the freedom to express childlike emotions without fear of reproof.

The boy in the barber shop

The other day I happened to be in a barber shop and across from me a little boy was clearly distressed about the idea of getting his hair cut. The barber proceeded to tell the boy that he should sit still, be quiet and stop being silly. It wasn't long before this little boy's distress became the focus of all the waiting customers.

At one point a gentleman offered the boy some chewing gum in an attempt to calm him down. The barber responded by saying 'he doesn't need a bubblegum – he needs a father! Where is the boy's father?' I had been trying hard to keep my focus on the book I was reading as I didn't want my eyes to be yet another pair fixated on this poor little boy – who by now had become quite a spectacle.

But eventually I did find myself looking up, hoping that the boy's mum, who had been sitting and listening to the whole thing, would come to his aid and offer him some reassurance and comfort. He was after all simply a child who was afraid about getting his hair cut. However, there was no reassurance, no acknowledgment of his fear and no one defended him against the torrent of snarling remarks being made about him and to him by the barber. I just sat there saying to myself, 'He is just a child…' It's amazing how we can so easily forget such an obvious fact, but sometimes we do miss the seemingly obvious: that a child in distress needs to be reassured not ridiculed.

Another thing that troubles me about this barber shop story is that in spite of what I know about children's needs and what I felt for the boy at the time, I didn't say anything. I'm not entirely sure why, but the fact is I did not put myself out for that little boy. It is of course much easier to advocate on a child's behalf in a professional setting where there is more clarity about our responsibility.

~

As teachers we need to consider what children may bring into school with them, not because they are 'naughty' or disturbed or challenged but simply because they are children. One sure thing about children is that they are not going to follow all of our instructions all of the time. Why? Because they are children.

Earlier in this chapter I mentioned that we are very much like children and I know that I certainly don't follow every instruction that is given to me; sometimes I am simply not in the mood, other times I may feel like testing the boundaries a bit. Be honest – do you do everything that you are told or asked to do?

You may argue that children should follow all of our instructions because we are the adults and they are the children and they should therefore do as we say. This is not a view that I share. If we want children to do as we say there are a number of things that we need to give thought to:

- Did I make the instruction clear?
- Did I ensure that I had the child's full attention before giving the instruction?
- Did I allow the child to ask questions for clarity?
- Did I speak in a tone that was congruent with what I was asking?
- Have I modelled the very response that I am now expecting?

As teachers we can be guilty of both expecting too much and accepting too little from children. At the end of it all, it's about us being gatekeepers; creating access points for all children to discover and realise their full potential in a safe environment where expectations are high but realistic.

Things to think about and do...

- How long do you expect children to be able to concentrate for?
- How much space do children have when sitting on the carpet?
- How comfortable is your classroom?
  - Is it too hot or too cold?
  - Are the chairs too small or too big?
  - Is the lesson stimulating?
  - Is there a sense of excitement and pace about the lesson?
- What might the children's behaviour be telling you about their preferred learning styles?

Chapter **Eight**

What will you do when behaviour gets to you?

Strategies for managing adult and child

One of the top reasons why teachers leave the profession is their inability to manage challenging behaviour. According to a survey in the *Times Educational Supplement* (*TES*) carried out by the General Teaching Council, 'Two in five NQTs desert the classroom because of workload and pupils' indiscipline.'

(*TES* Newspaper 11th July 2008)

After all, we are only human and we too have limitations. I'm hoping that this book has acknowledged just how emotive the issue of challenging behaviour can be, but more so, given you both help and hope.

Most of us can easily identify our Achilles' heel; the one thing that children do that really gets under our skin. I do an activity on this in my training sessions and always find it so interesting because people are very different. I call this part of the training 'Different Strokes, Different Folks'. It is fascinating that what would cause one teacher to become enraged would not bother another teacher at all.

One might say, 'I can't bear it when children fidget on the carpet.' While another will say, 'Oh no, for me, it's when they play with the Velcro on their shoes.' Then another one chimes in with, 'I can't stand it when children tell tales.' Yet, for someone else those are minor issues and they are more impacted by children who rock on their chairs. For me, the array of responses to this question highlights the importance of being aware of the things that children do that 'gets to you'.

Behaviour, as I have said in chapter five, is incredibly emotive and has the power to arouse strong feelings in even the most experienced professionals. Knowing what your Achilles' heel is allows you to be prepared and helps you to guard against inappropriate responses to these behaviours.

When colleagues have turned the question to me, asking, 'What is your Achilles' heel?' my response is lying and spitting. I have already told you a story about Allan, a former pupil of mine. Here is another one about him to illustrate this point.

Allan's Story – Part Two

It was around 2.30pm – what could possibly happen in the last forty-five minutes of the school day? As was often the case in the afternoon, Allan was struggling to stay focused and having already asked him a number of times to settle, I could see that he was becoming more and more agitated. My TA and I made eye contact and we knew what was about to happen – Allan was going to walk out of the classroom.

Allan had become too accustomed to simply walking out of lessons, rather than staying and applying the self-control needed to settle back to work. Walking out had become too easy for him, in my view, it was a soft option. That particular day, however, I'd already decided that I was not going to let him leave.

As I answered some of the children's questions, I slowly manoeuvred myself towards the door and stood next to my TA. It didn't need to be stated, she knew me well enough to know what I was planning. By now Allan was out of his seat and refusing to sit down. You could feel the agitation rising in him as I praised the rest of the class for keeping our rule of 'working hard and staying on task'. It was as if he was put out by the fact that the rest of the class just continued with their work. Having failed to receive the attention from the class that he had anticipated Allan, for the sake of his own pride, was now under pressure to take it to the next level and finish what he had started.

He was noticeably cautious as he circled the room and edged closer and closer to the door and there was something in his eyes that told me he knew his story would have a different ending that day. When I turned to make a comment to my TA, he made a quick grab for the door handle, but his hand was not as quick as my foot and I prevented the door from being opened. By now my whole body was in front of the door and Allan and I were face to face. I looked at him as he looked at me; the rest of the class were still and quiet.

The air was thick with anticipation. None of us – the class, Allan or I – had been here before and I'm sure we all had the same question on our minds, 'What is going to happen now?'

Allan stepped back, as if he had been caught unawares and needed more time to rethink his strategy. With measured aggression and desperation in his eyes, he ordered me to move out of the way. I looked at him and hoped that my face in some way reassured him of the motive for what I was doing. I didn't want him to feel the need to run anymore. I wanted him to know that even when he began to unravel and felt unsettled, he was still welcome in my classroom. I wanted him to know that my classroom and even more so my heart had room for him; in whatever state he found himself. What I couldn't say with my mouth I said with my eyes, *you don't have to run anymore Allan, this is a safe place.*

As we stood face to face, I simply said, 'You will not be leaving the classroom until three fifteen, like everyone else,' after which I directed my attention to the rest of the class and waited. Within the next few minutes Allan created two of my most memorable moments as a teacher…

By now the other pupils were getting packed up and ready for home. While I shadowed Allan, my TA was busy directing groups of children to go and get their coats and bags. Despite the frequent movement of children in and out of the classroom, Allan made no attempt to leave – as if he knew that this was a battle he was not going to win. Instead he turned his attention to the equipment in the classroom. He picked up a ruler and began to hit it against the table; then he moved his attention to the chairs and started throwing them onto the floor.

Having noticed that both I and the class were unmoved by his show he switched his attention to the children's work on display. The children gasped as he ripped a pathway through the middle of the display – I quickly moved in front of him and with a firm finger close to his face I stated, 'I will not allow you to destroy the children's work – this is their classroom too.'

As Allan jolted his head back he retorted, 'Don't point in my face with your sausage fingers!' The comment was so unexpected I nearly laughed out loud but I resisted as I didn't want Allan to think I was laughing at him.

By now the class had left and my TA and I had resorted to holding onto Allan because he was evidently not finished in his destruction of the display. The next thing he did, happened to be the one thing I had always hoped would never happen to me even as a behaviour specialist.

There was now genuine anger coming from Allan. He struggled and swore and shouted at the top of his voice, 'Let me go!'

My response was the same each time, 'I want to let you go, but I cannot let you go until you are calm.'

The headteacher entered the room and joined her voice to mine; reiterating the need for calm. Maybe it was the presence of another adult that made Allan do what he did next. Maybe another adult seeing him in this distressed state with tears streaming down his face was too much for him to bear. He tried one more time to jolt his hand from underneath mine and when that failed he leaned forward, pursed his lips and spat on the back of my hand. As the white froth slowly trickled down my hand and onto the floor a red mist quickly descended upon me, blurring my vision.

'Don't you dare spit at me!' I bellowed.

There was a shift in my tone, my disgust was palpable. There was a shift in the atmosphere too; my colleagues felt it, Allan felt it, I felt it. I released my grip. The space between Allan and I was now the principle thing because

I couldn't afford to be overtaken by the emotion of the moment. My colleagues stepped in, as I stepped out. I needed to get cleaned up; I needed to remove every trace of the one thing I hoped would never happen to me.

This incident had the potential to really rock my relationship with Allan. When a child hits your sore spot it can take a while to recover. A headteacher once said to me that he was surprised that I felt so strongly about being spat at. As if as a behaviour specialist I ought to be prepared to put up with anything. Behaviour experts have their limits like everyone else and it's about how we preserve our relationships with children when they push us to our limits. When you have children like Allan in your class you need three key things: support from colleagues, sound knowledge of the behaviour policy, and the capacity to forgive.

I can quite easily laugh at the Allan incident now as it is not every day that a child says you have 'sausage fingers'! In fact, my friends and I laughed about it for weeks afterwards. Particularly as one of them has always said I have 'podgy' fingers!

At the time though I knew I needed to distance myself; it was not about winning, it was about safety – both his and mine. I knew that type of behaviour would be appropriately dealt with by the headteacher, so I stepped back and allowed the policy to run its course. The policy clearly stated that verbal and physical abuse towards staff would not be tolerated and that incidents of that nature should be referred to the deputy or headteacher. Acknowledging my Achilles' heel helped me to be prepared in a difficult situation because I was already clear about my limits and what I needed to do when they were reached. Also knowledge of the agreed protocol helped me to know how to respond.

In these situations we should ensure our responses are proportionate to what has taken place. The child shouldn't have to bear the brunt of our frustrations because they have hit our sore spot. The obligation to remain calm, consistent and in control rests firmly with us and in the context of schools we never cease to be an institution of learning.

So, even in the midst of this difficult experience I still had to make sure that the incident served as a learning opportunity for Allan – not necessarily in that moment but certainly at some point. Often the learning opportunities get missed because there is so much emotion that the child leaves the situation having learnt nothing about their behaviour besides the fact that it has the potential to make adults very angry.

That incident was in fact the start of a major turning point for Allan. The refusal to let him run, the display of emotion from him and my ability to recover from this situation combined to create a positive shift in our relationship. Something about the incident communicated care to Allan: the fact that he was welcomed back into the class after a few days away from school.

As far as our relationship was concerned the incident was forgiven and forgotten. I did not hide my disappointment about what he had done and how he had behaved, but I was very clear to express disgust at what he had done and not at him. This is a fundamental key in our work and relationships with children: **separate the child from their behaviour.**

It brings me back to what I shared earlier about love. It was the decision that I had made about Allan when I was told about his behaviour, before I even met him, that enabled me to keep going. There were more attempts to walk out, a few more disruptions to lessons, but eventually he did settle into lessons.

I remember our first class assembly that Allan took part in. I caught sight of his mum at the back of the hall and the look of pride on her face was something I wanted to bottle and keep.

At the end of the assembly Allan said, 'I haven't taken part in a class assembly since year two.'

It certainly wasn't plain sailing with Allan after that, but he did manage to successfully complete the year in my class – much to many people's surprise.

Managing and Responding to Behaviour in the Classroom

Let us think a little more about the four misdirected goals of behaviour that I spoke about earlier in chapter three. Children's misbehaviour is generally about wanting to communicate one or more of these four things:

'I need your attention' (Attention seekers)

> '...Giving attention to attention-seeking children does not necessarily improve their behavior. When attention is given in response to children's misbehaviour, the misbehaviour increases. Although the search for attention is usually manifested in the form of misbehavior, even the cooperative behaviour of very young children may stem from a desire for special attention. Often, these children try to do better than others, and they are very sensitive to criticism and failure.'
>
> (Dreikurs, 1968, in Edwards, 2008, p.99)

We need to proceed with caution in our attempts to respond to a child's need for attention. As stated above, the risk is that we can actually end up feeding that need by giving too much attention to poor behaviour. It is important to remember that positive attention from a key adult is central to a child's development and is therefore a necessary element for even the most compliant child.

The key is to be very tactical about what you give your attention to, so as to avoid what I have seen time and time again during classroom observations: classrooms where the attention of the teacher is totally absorbed by children who exhibit challenging behaviour. As far as is possible keep your exchanges with these children short and, whenever you can, draw attention to children who are complying in order to bring other children into line.

Be aware of 'invisible' children otherwise we inadvertently give children the message that when you are well-behaved you are overlooked by adults. These are the children who comply with class rules day in and day out, but somehow are seldom seen or acknowledged. By using the strategies outlined below to deal with attention seekers, you also ensure that these compliant children get the recognition that they deserve for maintaining positive behaviour and for not allowing themselves to be distracted by the misbehaviour of others.

For example, if a child in your class calls out, rather than responding to them, you should say, 'Well done to the children who have remembered our rule about not calling out.' When the child corrects their behaviour, you then give them your attention and praise them for doing the right thing.

'I need to be in control' (Power seekers)

When dealing with power seekers, knowledge of the school rules and policy are important. These are the kinds of children who are prepared to take you on as a teacher by pushing the boundaries. For them the power and control they feel from the verbal exchange with you is what satisfies their need. When it comes to these children you need to use the language of the rules in a very scripted and repetitive way in order to avoid confrontation. These children need to understand that your feelings towards them are not personal, but that they have to comply with the rules like everyone else.

As hard as it may be, it can be very effective to give these children some legitimate control, by putting them in charge of something or giving them a little job around the class or around the school.

Please note, however, that these children will also seek to control their own failure. I have a story from my own teaching experience to illustrate this. I taught a boy in my year two class called Trenton. He was more streetwise than any other six-year-old I had ever met. His principle objective while in school was to preserve his street-cred and feed his need for control. If he got into trouble in class, he would say things like, 'Well call my mum then innit, just go and call my mum.' Or 'Just send me home man, send me home innit.'

In his mind, the fact that he was instructing us to send him home or call his mum, made him feel as though he was in control and that things were happening because he made them happen. He would often walk out of the classroom shortly after a reprimand because again it was about being in control; leaving the room because he chose to rather than being asked to.

For such behaviour the language of choice can be very effective as you can empower the child and place the choice in their hands. For example, in the case of Trenton I would say, 'It's your choice, you can come back and sit down or you will have to complete the work later, it's your choice.' It is very important to begin and end the statement with the words, 'it's your choice'.

This approach gives legitimate control to the child because they have the power to choose.

'I need you to feel as bad as I feel' (Revenge seekers)
Revenge seekers can be quite cruel and hurtful and it is vitally important to try and maintain a positive image of

these children. Again use the language of the rules rather than making it sound personal. At times revenge seekers will say things directly intended to cause hurt to children or adults; be sure to give these children opportunities to reflect on their behaviour and ensure that there are logical consequences to these types of behaviours.

For example, if a child hurt other children in the playground, the logical consequence would be for the child to be withdrawn from the playground, rather than withdrawn from class. Again, if a child emptied the contents of his tray onto the floor in a rage, the logical consequence would be for the child to have to use their time to clean it up. Logical consequences help the child to make the connection between the misbehaviour and the consequence. Children are also more likely to respond appropriately because the consequence is seen as fair and proportionate.

'I need to convince you not to expect anything from me' (Vulnerability seekers)

These children feel as though they have no one in their corner and low self-esteem is another common feature. Make more of a fuss about their successes than you do about their failures. Also set small, manageable targets, as well as helping them to develop small friendship groups where they can learn to build trust and esteem.

It is important to remember that what drives most behaviour is a genuine need, so the next section is about how you can legitimately meet the needs of children while directing and encouraging them towards more positive behaviour.

The following strategies are better suited to low level disruptions:

- **Tactical ignoring** – As far as is possible, ignore the negative behaviour that the child is exhibiting. Find a child who is sitting nearby and acknowledge the positive behaviour that they are demonstrating. What you are trying to do is to make clear what type of behaviour you will give your attention to.

    For example, if a child in your class is rocking from side to side, you might say to a child nearby, 'Carl, I love the way you are sitting still and looking this way.' You could also say, 'I'm looking for someone who is sitting still and looking this way… Well done Martin I can see you, well done Sarah I can see you…' Usually the child will amend their behaviour in order to get the same praise – however, when they do, it is very important that you notice and praise them for it. If they do not, then you need to proceed through your warning and sanctions system.

    By doing this you have tactically ignored the poor behaviour and made it clear to not just the individual child but to the class, the kind of behaviour that gets your attention. For attention seekers this is very important because they will come into your classroom having learnt a number of different ways of getting the attention of adults. This response is a positive way of helping a child to unlearn some of these behaviour habits.
- **Pick your battles** – Ask yourself, 'Is this really a big issue?' Another question to ask is, 'How much is this situation impacting the teaching and learning?' This has to be the bottom line in all classrooms: the impact on teaching and learning.

    When I am observing lessons, sometimes it is clear to see when a teacher's response to behaviour is more about them than it is about the class. Children are going to fidget – but does that mean that they are not learning? If it is not impacting your ability to teach and their capacity to learn, do we really need to draw attention to it? Sometimes it is the fact that we have drawn attention to it that actually disrupts the lesson!

It is not possible to correct every single child for every single thing that they do during lessons. The rules need to clearly state the agreed code of conduct and children need to be very clear about your expectations as a teacher. The last thing I will mention here is that it helps if we are prepared to do some self-analysis during or immediately after an incident to check that our responses are not about our mood or preferences. We need to be led by our professional responsibility and by the agreed policy.

- **Use the language of choice** – As part of our role as teachers we need to help children to understand the concept of cause and consequence. Using the language of choice makes this very explicit. So, rather than saying, 'You will miss your playtime if you do not do any work,' you would say, 'It's your choice, you can do the work now, or you will have to stay in at playtime to complete it. It's your choice.' Here's another example: 'You will go to the timeout corner if you do not stop talking.' Instead you would say, 'It's your choice, you can stop talking or you will have to go to the timeout corner. It's your choice.'

  Using the language of choice is empowering and places the responsibility of fixing the behaviour on the child. This is very significant for power seekers. It also communicates to children that making mistakes is normal and that they can be remedied with the right choice.
- **Be clear** – State your expectations at regular intervals throughout the day and throughout a lesson. Before setting children off on a task, tell them what you expect and what you will be looking for. Clear expectations leave little room for misbehaviour. Once you have

made things clear, you can then hold children to account because they know exactly what they should be doing.

- **Be consistent** – If you say that children should not talk while you are talking then that is how it should be all the time, every time. Do not settle for a quiet hum while you are talking to the class, insist on their full attention.
- **Use humour** – Is there a way you can appropriately make light of a situation? Someone once said, 'As a general rule, the freedom of any people can be judged by the volume of their laughter.'
- **Be aware and informed** – What are the rules? What are the routines? What are the agreed rewards and sanctions? Is there a change to the timetable that you need to communicate to the children to circumvent any disruptions?
- **Remember, relationships are fundamental** – Rules without relationships breed rebellion. It is so important to build relationships and trust with children, so that when sanctions need to be applied children know that they are being issued from a position of genuine care, not in an attempt to be punitive and hostile.

~

We do not have the privilege of choosing the kinds of children that come across the thresholds of our schools and to be honest I am not sure that I would want to. The beautiful mosaic that is the inner city classroom is a challenging but incredibly rewarding setting within which to work.

In closing, the thought that comes to mind is of a group of children playing hide and seek. You know the drill – a group go off to hide, while one child stands and counts. When the child has finished counting they say, 'coming, ready or not!' Children are pouring into our schools with all sorts of issues that our teacher training did not adequately prepare us for.

They are coming whether we are ready or not. Isn't it our duty, both to them and for own sense of competence and satisfaction, to do everything within our power to be better prepared to meet them, to reach them, and to teach them?

Things to think about and do...

- What is your Achilles' heel?
- Are you clear about the process in your school for dealing with extreme behaviour?
- Are your classroom rules displayed in a place where they can be seen and referred to regularly?

Chapter Nine

Do they know the two Rs?

Rules and routines

A child's need for structure and predictability is vital if they are to be free from fear and able to be an effective learner. This chapter simply serves as a reminder about the significance of rules and routines as a means of providing children with the boundaries that they need in order to thrive.

Abraham Maslow, the American Psychologist, developed a theory about our needs as humans. It is known in both education and psychology circles as: Maslow's Hierarchy of Human Needs.

Some people believe that Maslow's Hierarchy of Human Needs has lost its relevance, but I believe that what he had to say about our need for safety and security is very significant in our work with children.

Maslow's Hierarchy of Human Needs

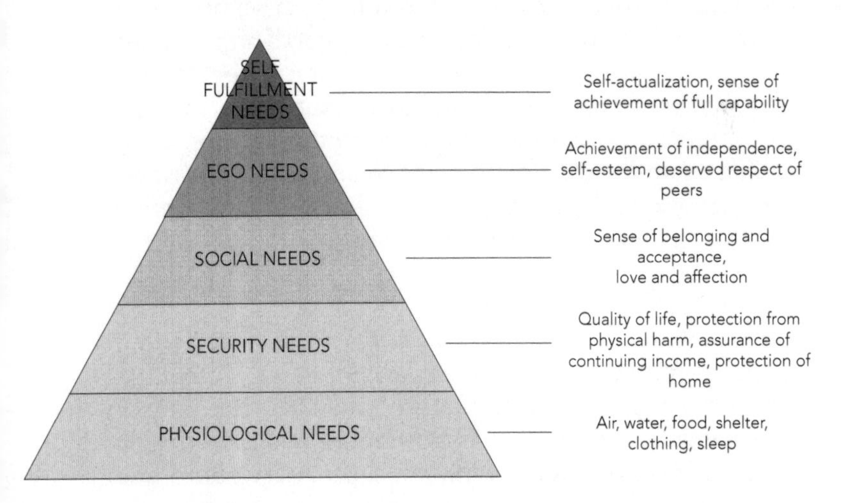

He identified a hierarchy of basic needs. They are portrayed in the shape of a pyramid, with the largest and most fundamental level of needs at the bottom. The idea is that when one level of need is met, physiological needs being the most important, the individual will then begin to feel a level of desire and motivation towards fulfilling the other needs. For example, someone who lacks food, employment and friends, would consider their need for food to be the most important.

When it comes to children the need for safety and security cannot be overstated. It is an accepted truth that children function best where there is safety – both physical and emotional, structure, stability, predictability and consistency. It is when these fundamentals are in place that children can really thrive because they are free from anxiety and fear.

Routines are extremely important because they help to establish the kind of predictability where children know the agreed order of things. In the context of schools, a lot of low level disruption can be circumvented if firm routines are put in place. For example, if the established routine is that children come into the classroom and get straight on with the work on the board during the register, there is little room for children to come in and create their own entertainment during the register because the routine enables the teacher to avoid that problem.

Rights, Rules and Routines

Dealing with challenging behaviour is no easy feat and it is therefore of the utmost importance that we protect the rights of children, in spite of their behaviour. Our duty of care extends to even the most disruptive and problematic children that we could possibly come across. I would argue that children for whom challenging behaviour has become a regular habit, need our love and protection the most, though some would argue that they deserve it the least.

In some cases these children come from homes where structure and routines are lacking and they crave the kind of safety that classrooms and school structures have the potential to provide.

It is worth adding here, that in spite of this need for structure, children can still find it difficult to comply because although they like the feeling of safety that comes from school structures and routines, they do not, however, welcome the constraints that are placed on them. This aspect of rules and routines can take a little getting used to.

Children have a number of rights when it comes to education and the quality of that provision. They have a right to a positive environment in which to work and learn. They have rights to respect and dignity, to feel physically and emotionally safe. These rights could easily apply to all members of the school community.

School rules set out the agreed protocol for working and interacting together in a school setting. Rules are the principles that govern conduct. They safeguard you, so that your language and actions are not rooted in emotion, but rooted in policy.

Another definition from the *Collins Dictionary*:

-pol-i-cy;

1. course of **action** adopted

You will notice the use of the word 'action' in the definition because a policy should be lived out by the individuals who are governed by it. The policy provides guidance and sets out the agreed expectations. Once we have read it and understood it, we should be running with it – putting it into practice. The idea of policy should not be the thought of a folder tucked away in a cupboard somewhere, it should actually be a set of expectations that we are fully acquainted with and committed to living out in our day to day work.

Rules are of primary importance because they protect rights, promote responsibility and describe the good behaviour that the adults within a school want to see.

Establishing rules

Rules need to be:

- **Simple and clear** – Be careful with words like 'respect', 'be good', 'always' or 'never'. Your choice of words should be clear and leave no room for question or debate. Children should not be left thinking 'what is respect?' or 'what is meant by being good?' 'Always' is a word to avoid because, in reality, no one whether adult or child is going to 'always' do one thing or another. Children are going to make mistakes and need to feel as though they can do so and quickly recover.

  Five is a good number for rules or at the most six. They should be simply stated, concise and easy to remember.
- **Positively phrased** – So rather than, 'we will not waste working time', the rule would state, 'we will work hard and stay on task'. Rather than, 'we will not speak horribly to one another', the rule should state 'we will use positive words and not put downs'.

  The rules should describe the behaviour you want to see rather than state what children should avoid.
- **Discussed and agreed with children** – As far as is possible, children should be a part of the establishment of rules. They should help with the wording and understand why particular rules are necessary. This process helps adults to get the buy-in they need from children because instead of feeling dictated to they become a vital part of an important decision making process.

- **Workable in the classroom environment** – They should relate to classroom activity and cover the full range of things that happen there such as:

  - How to work
  - How to communicate – with each other and with the teacher
  - How to interact with one another
  - How and when to move around
  - How to regard property – both school and personal

  The best example of school rules is where one set of rules exists for the whole school. For example, in one school I worked in, the school rules were referred to as the 'Going for Gold Rules'. This one set of rules governed the conduct throughout all aspects of school life: the dining hall, the playground and the classroom. They were clearly visible in every classroom, in corridors, in the dining hall and in the playground.
- **Referred to regularly** – The rules should be talked about and referred to daily and at varying junctures throughout the day. Children and adults should know the rules and be able to quote them with ease. As I discussed earlier, how can you live out a policy if you do not know what it says? The language of the rules should be used when praising or correcting children. Take the following set of school rules as an example:

  1. We take care of school property
  2. We stay on task in lessons
  3. We share our equipment and ideas
  4. We take turns to speak
  5. We say things that are helpful and kind

With these rules in mind, here are some examples of the type of language you would adopt to reinforce the rules daily in your classroom:

- 'Excellent 5T – everyone is on task in our lesson.'
- 'Thank you Susie for waiting for your turn to speak.'
- 'Well done for picking up that pencil off of the floor Brian – our rule is "we look after property".'

When correcting children or reissuing warnings:

- 'Rebecca this is a warning because you are not on task.'
- 'We say things that are kind and helpful Tom, what you said was hurtful. Please go to the timeout area.'
- 'Sarah, please do not hide the rubbers because in this school we share our equipment.'

Using the language of the rules helps you to be consistent when speaking to children about their behaviour. It also keeps the rules present in people's minds and vocabulary – it provides a constant reminder about expectations and reinforces the agreed code of conduct.

Routines

Routines are a sequence of actions regularly followed that enable the rules to be held firmly in place. They enable the rules to work. This sequence of actions provides structure and predictability for children. It can be quite daunting for any of us to be in a situation where we cannot predict what will happen next.

For example, when you arrive at a station to discover the train line you use is not operating, you feel somewhat thrown because it disrupts your routine. In the same respect, if you travelled home by bus and it took an unexpected diverted route, it can be both annoying and distressing because there is something about the safety of routine that helps us to be free from fear and anxiety. Children are no different and they do not simply want, rather they need routine.

When routines are changed it is very important, as far as is possible, to let children know in advance. What is a minor change for an adult could be a major change for a child. For example, if an adult who usually works in your class is not going to be in, let the children know. Or if you have decided to make some changes to the timetable, again, let the children know.

In your classroom try to have clear structures and routines for:

- **Coming into the classroom** – What do they do on entry?
  - Stand behind chairs?
  - Hang up coats and go straight to the carpet?
  - Get straight on with the work on the board?
- **Leaving the classroom** – How do they exit the classroom?
  - Table by table or group by group?
  - Line up at the door or go straight out?
- **Moving around** – Who goes where?
  - Are there areas that are out of bounds to children?
  - Who gets equipment if needed?
  - How many children can sharpen pencils at one time?
- **Getting their attention** – How will they know what you want?
  - Will you clap your hands?
  - Will you ring a bell?
  - Will you shake a tambourine?
  - Will you raise your hand?

Other things that will require thought and planning are routines for packing away. Who does it and how does it happen? Many teachers have a certain type of pack down music. I saw a year two teacher use the theme tune for 'Mission Impossible' for pack down time and as soon as the children heard it, they knew exactly what to do. Within seconds they were moving around like an army of ants, getting the classroom packed up. It was great!

You will also need to consider where children sit in the classroom. Seat them where they are likely to learn best. Also consider rotating the seating arrangements as it can be a bit of an ordeal being stuck next to the same person for an entire year, especially in primary schools!

The routines that I personally use vary according to the year group I teach, but here are some examples and my reasoning behind them:

- **Children stand behind their chairs on entry to the classroom** – This helps to settle the children when they arrive in the morning or re-enter the classroom after lunch break. Once they are behind their chairs and they are quiet, I greet them and then we get stuck into learning. It seems to in some way set the tone for learning to begin.
- **'Rocket arm'** – This is where I hold my hand straight up in the air to indicate that I want the attention of the class. The children see my arm and then do likewise until it is 'caught' by everyone. In some cases I have added a verbal cue, particularly if children are in the midst of quite a vibrant activity. I may hold my hand up and say 'Ok year five, I need your attention, thank you Mikey, thank you Sarah', and so on.
- **Pack down music** – I tend to go for pack down music because as soon as the children hear it, they know exactly what to do. It also makes packing away feel

like less of a drag and things get done efficiently with a little singing and dancing along the way!

- **Table monitors** – I generally do not allow children to get up and walk around the classroom. Each table has a monitor who is in charge of table equipment. At the end of the day the table monitor sharpens all the pencils and makes sure that all the table equipment is in place for the next day. These monitors are rotated on a weekly basis. This helps to make the classroom feel more purposeful because there is no unnecessary movement. It can be very unsightly to walk into a classroom where children are strolling around as if they are out on a sight-seeing tour!

When it comes to the alphabet, there is an established order, b follows a all the time, every time. In short, routines are an agreed understanding about how and when things happen. Children thrive on predictability, structure and routine. There is a place for spontaneity, particularly in our work as teachers, but children need routines. So do not think that you are depriving your children by giving them structure and routine; it is vital to their development.

Sometimes, however, things may have to change but these changes need to be explained. Be sure to let children see that even when things do not go according to plan, you still have a level of control and show the children that you have managed it. Acknowledge your own inconsistencies when it comes to routines and own the response of the children. If things have been a little inconsistent, you will need to be patient with the children as you try to re-set things.

Routines can also help to eliminate the power struggle both within the home and at school. Things happen, not because adults are being mean, but because it is simply the agreed time for that activity to take place, whether it is brushing teeth, going to bed, packing away or coming in from outside. Having an established routine can make all the difference to your stress levels and to the children's feeling of safety.

Things to think about and do...

◆ When we talk about safety, we forget that emotional safety is just as important if not more important than physical safety. Take some time now to reflect on these questions:

- How safe do your children feel around you?
- Are your moods predictable?
- Are you approachable?
- Are your responses to them measured and appropriate?
- Do your children feel a sense of belonging in your classroom?

◆ How will you deal with the things that need to be improved?

Chapter Ten

Can you show me as well as tell me?

Teaching positive behaviour; what they should do as well as what they shouldn't

I am hoping that by now you will agree with me that all behaviour is about something. It has a place from which it has come (the root) and a place where it would like to go (the goal). For children who have learnt over time to display behaviours in order to get their needs met, there is a need for much support and encouragement in order to help them to unlearn those habits. It is very important that we understand what we are asking of these children when we say, 'don't do this' or 'stop doing that'.

For this reason we do not simply correct poor behaviour but teach appropriate behaviour. We need to give children alternative ways to communicate, to interact and to get their essential needs for attention and control met.

This is why positive behaviour must be taught and modelled, as some children will take attention however they can get it. When we say to children 'don't do this, don't do that', we must offer children alternative behaviours otherwise we strip them of their defences and leave them exposed.

By that I mean some children have worked hard at mastering behaviours and attitudes which they know will elicit a response from adults. The reality for both adults and children is that by the time our behaviours have become habitual, we are receiving some degree of benefit from them; there is a payoff otherwise the behaviours would not be worthwhile. So, understand what you are asking when you tell a child to stop doing what they have always done – for the child that is a big request.

It is important that our approach to these children is balanced; that we have genuine relationships which allow us to engage with them in a meaningful way and not just when we need to address them about their behaviour. We do not want to reinforce the message that poor behaviour brings adult attention.

A conscious effort is needed to build relationships with these children outside of their behaviour. It is about intentionality. On occasions, when they are doing the right thing, adults need to notice and celebrate a child's achievements. It is these children who need mentors and key workers; not someone who will add to the numerous voices telling them off. They need an adult who is intentionally building relationship, intentionally investing and enquiring about them as individuals.

Thinking back to the barber shop story, what was really interesting about that episode was when the young boy eventually settled down and sat still long enough for his hair to be cut, no one seemed to notice. No voice could be heard praising him for turning his behaviour around and doing the right thing. The silence was a stark contrast to the many voices which had earlier berated and scoffed at him.

Teaching Positive Behaviour – How Does it Work?

The first step is to acknowledge the need to not only 'preach' about behaviour but also to teach positive behaviour. I have heard it said that positive behaviour should be 'caught' as well as taught. Adults should model the very behaviours they expect from children: saying please and thank you (it sounds obvious, but you would be very surprised how many people forget even the most basic common courtesies in their dealings with children), not talking over children, respecting their personal space, and saying sorry – to name but a few.

The next step is to examine your thoughts towards these children as how you feel will affect your motivation to teach positive behaviour. Consider the following:

- How do you feel about the most challenging child in your class or school? If you do not have a positive regard for these children, you will not be inclined to want to teach them anything.
- Are you likely to teach them positive behaviour if you do not believe that their behaviour can or will change?

- What if you do not regard the child as your problem?
- What happens when you are just holding out for the child to move to another class?

You can make a firm decision about how you are going to 'be' and how you are going to 'see' these children. Teaching positive behaviour is rooted in intentionality. It is born out of a genuine desire to help these children learn, grow and maximise their potential. For adults in schools it is part of our professional responsibility.

Before I move on, I'll repeat an earlier appeal – please do not lose sight of the child in the midst of their behaviour. Please do not forget that they are still on the journey of working out who to be and how to be and that with the help and commitment of caring adults, they will get there. Be the One to contradict their view of themselves as being unworthy and unsuccessful. Be the One to contradict their view of adults as being uncaring and hostile. It only takes One – one person and one decision – to bring a change to a young life. **You can't be something to everybody – but you can be everything to somebody.**

Give equal if not more time to teaching positive behaviour than you do to correcting negative behaviour

Try to get into the habit of not simply stating what you don't want but being descriptive about what positive behaviour looks like. A few examples:

Avoid saying...	An alternative...
Don't talk so loud	Use a quiet voice in the classroom
Stop running in the corridor	Walk in the corridor please
I don't want to see snatching and arguing during the group work	I'm looking for people sharing ideas and resources
Don't shout out on the carpet	Put your hand up and wait patiently

When dealing with a behaviour incident ensure there is time allocated to talking through the incident with the child in question – this is when both the teaching of positive behaviour and the learning from negative behaviour takes place. Help the child to understand the impact of their behaviour on others.

For example, say, 'When you called Lucas an idiot, you hurt his feelings and made him feel sad.' Also help the child to contribute their ideas as to how the situation could be rectified. Perhaps ask, 'What can we do to make things better?' Another good question to ask is, 'What do you think you need to do next time?' Here's the key – when that 'next time' does come around be sure to notice when the child does deal with it more appropriately.

Behaviour management strategies do not work in isolation; you cannot simply apply these strategies in a mechanical and sterile fashion. The principle thing will always be the quality of your relationships with individual children.

When you are teaching children about positive behaviour you need to wait until you are calm enough to be able to engage in the conversation; so that the child catches the lesson and not just the emotion. Similarly, children are most likely to listen if they get the sense that you are genuinely interested in helping them.

Let the children know you expect the best from them
If we have no expectation that children can change, how can we effectively teach positive behaviour? When children make the wrong choice about how to respond, don't be angry – be disappointed. This is much more effective because it communicates to the child that you expect better from them.

When you are giving children instructions or warnings, add a 'thank you' at the end – it communicates that you are expecting compliance from the child. For example, say, 'Go back to your seat please Billy, thank you.' The 'thank you' communicates faith in their ability to do the right thing. It's simple, but effective.

Another way to communicate high expectations for behaviour is by positively reintegrating a child back into class after timeout. Too often children return to class after timeout to find that their teacher is still angry and hostile towards them, even though they have taken their sanction. This may make the adult feel satisfied but it does little to help the situation or the relationship. Teachers sometimes make the mistake of thinking this is what is required; that they must show their disdain for the inappropriate behaviour for a prolonged time. Children interpret it as being directed at them and it causes them to feel unsettled because in their minds you are still angry and in that context it can be difficult to settle back into learning.

Alternatively, it helps if first of all you notice that the child has returned and secondly you communicate some sort of expectation that the remainder of the day or session is going to be positive. For example, you could say, 'Welcome back Rachel. Please go back to your seat. I look forward to coming and looking at some of your work before you go to break.' This type of welcome goes a long way towards communicating to the child that you have moved on from the incident, that the child has a second chance and that their relationship with you is still intact. What can add real weight to this is if you also look for an opportunity to praise the child for positive behaviour following their return. So if the child returns and settles, notice and praise them for it.

Use positive statements to make expectations explicit
What constitutes positive behaviour needs to be made very clear to children, so they know what is required and how they can do more of it. When you are praising children be very specific regarding what you are pleased about so that the child knows what they have done well and can therefore repeat it on another occasion. It can help to use positive statements such as:

- 'I like the way you are working as a team.'
- 'I like the way you are taking it in turns to speak in your group.'
- 'I am pleased with you because you put your hand up.'
- 'I enjoyed your...'
- 'I feel happy when you...'
- 'I love the way you are...'
- 'I can see you are trying really hard...'

Praise needs to be frequent and specific. For example, don't just say 'well done', say 'well done for waiting your turn'. Make sure you are clear about what you mean when you say things like 'be good' or 'be sensible'. Remember to praise effort as well as achievement – if you have asked the class to tidy up, even if they are reluctantly complying, praise their efforts as they press towards completion.

A word of caution about praise: be careful not to devalue praise by giving it too readily for things that are not 'praiseworthy'. Praise should be used to affirm your expectations and acknowledge the efforts of children at both ends of the scale: those who exhibit positive behaviour consistently as well as those for whom positive behaviour is a huge challenge. I am not advocating the use of praise to win children over.

Try to avoid over-praising children for doing things that they should be doing regardless. For example, children shouldn't necessarily be rewarded or praised for simply reading out their work in class or for tidying up after themselves.

Have clear and firm boundaries

Children learn the dos and don'ts of behaviour when the boundary lines are clearly stated. In much the same way that the laws of our land clearly set out the accepted way of behaving and indeed the penalties for non-compliance; children similarly need clarity about how far they can go and it needs to be established in advance what will happen when the 'laws' are broken. Consistency is paramount.

Both in classrooms and at home too, adults need to be clear about what they will and will not accept from children. Where there has been deterioration in behaviour because of a lack of consistency on the part of the adults, these mistakes need to be owned by the adults in question and quickly rectified. There is of course room for flexibility – you can bend a rule, but don't break it.

Schools never stop being institutions of learning and teaching positive behaviour is as important as teaching Maths and English. When we as teachers get this right, the reverberations are felt for generations of children.

Things to think about and do...

- Children will have acquired habitual behaviours over a period of years; change will therefore not be instant.
- Children need to be told and retold, repetition is key.
- Use visuals to teach children about appropriate behaviours, try not to rely solely on language based approaches.

Conclusion

How will they know?

I was unwavering in my decision not to write a book that simply listed the dos and don'ts of behaviour management. One thing I have learnt is that when it comes to talking about behaviour, you have to engage people's hearts because a change of heart on the part of a teacher can lead to a changed life for a child. That is what I am hoping I have done here – influenced change in your heart concerning how you look at children who exhibit challenging behaviour.

In fact not just how you look at them, but how you look at yourself in relation to them and the potential you have to be a part of a turning point in their young lives. A similar turning point to the one created by my own teacher which has led to me writing this book and sharing my story with you. Had I not met her, I honestly do not know if you would be meeting me through this book.

I have shared my story about the impact a teacher had on my life, but what story will the children in your school share about you? In reality you are writing a little bit of that story every day. For our children the story of their little lives has already begun and we had no control over their beginnings. However, the opportunity now awaits us to use what we now know to help a child create a picture of a preferred future; a picture that is full of colour and light.

This book is simply a reminder of what we fundamentally know to be true about the power of positive relationships. When people believe in us it does something on the inside. It spurs us on, it helps us to get up when we fall down; slowly but surely we start to believe that we can do better. So I'm suggesting a return to what we know.

How will your children know that you have read this book? How will they know that you have made the decision to return to your promises? What is going to be different? The **realisation** that you need to be the One is step 1; the **decision** to be the One is step 2; but the **action** that you commit to taking as a result of your realisation and decision is step 3. It's only when you get to step 3 that the children really begin to feel the impact because things actually change. You move from talking a good talk to walking the kind of walk that brings positive change to little lives.

I wholeheartedly believe that what children with challenging behaviour need is for someone to be the One. They need someone to be courageous enough to answer the call. Their behaviour calls to us from classrooms, schools and neighbourhoods, and it says, 'Will You be the One?'

I will leave you with the words of my poem. I hope that it will inspire you to apply what you have learnt from this book.

'Will You be the One?'

Will You hold my hand
and tell me that I can?
Will You say yes, when others say no?
Will You stay, while others go?
Will You stand on the sidelines cheering my name?
Encouraging me to stay in the game?
Will You take the time to hear me out?
Speak to me without the need to shout?

Will You notice the good as well as the bad?
You see I come with more than a pen and pad.
I try to shut them out but they follow me to class,
the sound of screams and breaking glass.
I try to focus… '5 + 5 makes 10'.
But then I wonder 'Will mummy and daddy be fighting again?'
At least I got some questions right in my test,
but then my teacher said I didn't try my best.

Alone in my world, I sit and stare;
no one seems to have an ear to hear.
Isn't there anyone prepared to hear me out?
Someone who wonders what my behaviour's about?
Teachers, TAs, counsellors and mentors,
in their own unique way pointing out my flaws.
There's a new sound that I long to hear.
The sound of hope, telling me that change is near.
Searching for a hero, but I can't find none,
Seems a good place to ask a question…

Will **You** be the One?

Bibliography and References

Canter, L (2001) Assertive Discipline: Solution Tree, USA

Collins Shorter Dictionary and Thesaurus (1991) Harper Collins Publishers, London

Cowley, S (2006) Getting the Buggers to Behave: Continuum International Publishing Group, London

Delaney, M (2009) Teaching the Unteachable: Worth Publishing Ltd, London

Edwards, H C (2008) Classroom Discipline and Management: John Whiley & Sons Inc, USA

Fox, J (2010) 'Building Resilience': Child Centered Practice

Ginott, G H (1975) Teacher and Child: Avon Books, USA

Goleman, D (1995) Emotional Intelligence: Bloomsbury Publishing Plc, London

Maslow H A, Frager D R, Fadiman J (1997) Motivation and Personality: Pearson, London

Mehrabian & Ferris (1967) 'Inference of attitudes from nonverbal communication in two channels', Journal of Consulting Psychology, 31, (3), p.248-252

Rogers & McPherson (2008) Behaviour Management with Young Children: SAGE Publications Ltd, London

Tauber, T R (2007) Classroom Management Sound Theory and Effective Practice: Praeger Publishers, USA

Webster-Stratton, C (2005) The Incredible Years: Incredible Years, USA

I am grateful to the individuals who gave their permission to reproduce copyright material. In some instances I have been unable to trace the owners of copyright material and would appreciate any information that would enable me to do so.

About the Author

Tracey Campbell is the Director and Lead Trainer of Be the One Transforming Behaviour Ltd, which partners with schools to provide training, consultancy and coaching in all areas of behaviour management. The organisation offers training for parents and supports children to address the issues of social and emotional development that give rise to challenging behaviour.

She has over fifteen years' experience working with children and young people in the UK and abroad. Beginning her career as a primary school teacher Tracey's perceptive approach resulted in her becoming a Lead Behaviour Professional within her NQT year. Tracey qualified as an Advanced Skills Teacher in Behaviour Management in 2009. In this role she supported schools by providing model lessons for colleagues in classroom practice and behaviour management. Her outreach work included the delivery of INSETs and coaching in Positive Behaviour Management.

She designed and delivers an inspirational behaviour management training series entitled 'Will You be the One?' which featured as part of the Investing in Diversity Programme at the Institute of Education.

To make contact with Tracey Campbell or to enquire about the work of Be the One Transforming Behaviour Ltd please visit:

www.bethe1.org.uk